TEACHER'S PET PUBLICATIONS

LitPlan Teacher Pack™
for
The Devil's Arithmetic
based on the book by
Jane Yolen

Written by Janine H. Sherman

TABLE OF CONTENTS - *The Devil's Arithmetic*

A FEW NOTES ABOUT THE AUTHOR
Jane Yolen

YOLEN, Jane (1939-). Jane Yolen grew up in New York City , the daughter of two writers. She attended Smith College and received her master's degree in education from the University of Massachusetts. She has taught children's literature at Smith and is the wife of Professor David W. Stemple. They have three grown children- all of whom have done books with her - and a brand new grandchild. The distinguished author of more than 170 books, Jane Yolen is a person of many talents. When she is not writing, she composes songs, travels, teaches, and is a professional storyteller on stage.

All of Yolen's stories and poems are somehow rooted in her sense of family and self. The 1983 Caldecott Honor Book, *The Emperor and the Kite*, was based on Yolen's relationship with her late father who was an international kite-flying champion. Her 1988 Caldecott Medal winner, *Owl Moon*, was inspired by her husband's interest in birding. Jewish Book Award and Association of Jewish Libraries Award winner, *The Devil's Arithmetic*, is a unique time-travel story of the Holocaust. When asked what got her interested in the subject she said, "Both sides of my family came over at the beginning of this century and we had no family left in either the Ukraine or Latvia during World War II. I am interested in the Holocaust as a Jew and as a citizen of the world." Other award winning books include: *The Girl Who Loved the Wind, Piggins, The Seeing Stick*, and *Commander Toad in Space.*

Throughout her writing career she has remained true to her primary source of inspiration- folk culture. Folklore is the "perfect second skin," writes Yolen, "From under its hide, we can see all the shimmering, shadowy uncertainties of the world. It is the universal human language, a language that children instinctively feel in their hearts." Perhaps the best explanation for her outstanding accomplishments come from Yolen herself: "I don't care whether the story is real or fantastical. I tell the story that needs told."

Yolen's versatility has led her to be called America's Hans Christian Anderson and the Aesop of the 20th century. This gifted and natural storyteller's books have been translated into twelve languages.

INTRODUCTION - *Devil's Arithmetic*

This unit has been designed to develop students' reading, writing, thinking, and language skills through exercises and activities related to *The Devil's Arithmetic* by Jane Yolen. It includes twenty lessons, supported by extra resource materials.

The **introductory lesson** introduces students to background information about places, people, and events mentioned throughout this novel. It also doubles as the first writing assignment for the unit. Following the introductory activity, students are given an explanation of how the activity relates to the book they are about to read. Following the transition, students are given the materials they will be using during the unit.

The **reading assignments** are approximately twenty -five pages each; some are a little shorter while others are a little longer. Students have approximately 15 minutes of Pre-reading work to do prior to each reading assignment. This Pre-reading work involves reviewing the study questions for the assignment and doing some vocabulary work for 10 or more vocabulary words they will encounter in their reading.

The **study guide questions** are fact-based questions; students can find the answers to these questions right in the text. These questions come in two formats: short answer or multiple choice. The best use of these materials is probably to use the short answer version of the questions as study guides for students (since answers will be more complete), and to use the multiple choice version for occasional quizzes. If your school has the appropriate machinery, it might be a good idea to make transparencies of your answer keys for the overhead projector.

The **vocabulary work** is intended to enrich students' vocabularies as well as to aid in the students' understanding of the book. Prior to each reading assignment, students will complete a two-part worksheet for the vocabulary words in the upcoming reading assignment. Part I focuses on students' use of general knowledge and contextual clues by giving the sentence in which the word appears in the text. Students are then to write down what they think the words mean based on the words' usage. Part II nails down the definitions of the words by giving students dictionary definitions `of the words and having students match the words to the correct definitions based on the words' contextual usage. Students should then have a thorough understanding of the words when they meet them in the text.

After each reading assignment, students will go back and formulate answers for the study guide questions. Discussion of these questions serves as a **review** of the most important events and ideas presented in the reading assignments.

After students complete extra discussion questions, there is a **vocabulary review** lesson which pulls together all of the fragmented vocabulary lists for the reading assignments and gives students a review of all of the words they have studied.

Following the reading of the book, two lessons are devoted to the **extra discussion questions/writing assignments/activities**. These questions focus on interpretation, critical analysis and personal response, employing a variety of thinking skills and adding to the students' understanding of the novel. These questions are done as a **group activity**. Using the information they have acquired so far through individual work and class discussions, students get together to further examine the text and to brainstorm ideas relating to the themes of the novel.

The group activity is followed by a **reports and discussion/activity** session in which the groups share their ideas about the book with the entire class; thus, the entire class gets exposed to many different ideas regarding the themes and events of the book.

There are three **writing assignments** in this unit, each with the purpose of informing, persuading, or having students express personal opinions. The first assignment is to inform: students write a composition about one of the background topics assigned in Lesson One. The second assignment gives students the opportunity to express personal opinion: students will keep a diary throughout the reading of the novel. The third assignment gives students the chance to persuade: students will pretend to be Hannah (Chaya) in the camp when the commandant comes and sees Reuven limping out of the camp hospital. Her objective is to convince Breuer not to choose Reuven.

The **nonfiction reading assignment** is tied in with Writing Assignment 1 and the introductory lesson. Students are required to read a piece of nonfiction related in some way to *The Devil's Arithmetic*. In this case, the topics are assigned in Lesson One. After reading their nonfiction pieces, students will fill out a worksheet on which they answer questions regarding facts, interpretation, criticism, and personal opinions. During one class period, students make **oral presentations** about the nonfiction pieces they have read. This not only exposes all students to a wealth of information, it also gives students the opportunity to practice **public speaking**.

The **review lesson** pulls together all of the aspects of the unit. The teacher is given four or five choices of activities or games to use which all serve the same basic function of reviewing all of the information presented in the unit.

The **unit test** comes in two formats: all multiple choice-matching-true/false or with a mixture of matching, short answer, and composition. As a convenience, two different tests for each format have been included.

There are additional **support materials** included with this unit. The **extra activities** section includes suggestions for an in-class library, crossword and word search puzzles related to the novel, and extra vocabulary worksheets. There is a list of **bulletin board ideas** which gives the teacher suggestions for bulletin boards to go along with this unit. In addition, there is a list of **extra class activities** the teacher could choose from to enhance the unit or as a substitution for an exercise the teacher might feel is inappropriate for his/her class. **Answer keys** are located directly after the **reproducible student materials** throughout the unit. The student materials may be reproduced for use in the teacher's classroom without infringement of copyrights. No other portion of this unit may be reproduced without the written consent of Teacher's Pet Publications, Inc.

UNIT OBJECTIVES - *The Devil's Arithmetic*

1. Through reading Jane Yolen's, *The Devil's Arithmetic*, students will gain appreciation for the importance of cultural and family traditions.

2. Students will acquire an understanding of the value of bearing witness.

3. Students will do background research to familiarize themselves with the Yiddish language and the plight of the Jews during the World War II era.

4. Students will be exposed to atrocities and horrors of the Holocaust.

5. Students will gain appreciation for and demonstrate proficiency in identifying and using figurative language.

6. Students will demonstrate their understanding of the text on four levels: factual, interpretive, critical and personal.

7. Students will be given the opportunity to practice reading aloud and silently to improve their skills in each area.

8. Students will define their own viewpoints on the aforementioned themes and answer questions to demonstrate their knowledge and understanding of the main events and characters in *The Devil's Arithmetic* as they relate to the author's theme development.

9. Students will enrich their vocabularies and improve their understanding of the novel through the vocabulary lessons prepared for use in conjunction with the novel.

10. The writing assignments in this unit are geared to several purposes:
    a. To have students demonstrate their abilities to inform, to persuade, or to express their own personal ideas
    > Note: Students will demonstrate ability to write effectively to <u>inform</u> by developing and organizing facts to convey information. Students will demonstrate the ability to write effectively to <u>persuade</u> by selecting and organizing relevant information, establishing an argumentative purpose, and by designing an appropriate strategy for an identified audience. Students will demonstrate the ability to write effectively to <u>express personal ideas</u> by selecting a form and its appropriate elements.
    b. To check the students' reading comprehension
    c. To make students think about the ideas presented by the novel
    d. To encourage logical thinking

READING ASSIGNMENT SHEET - *The Devil's Arithmetic*

Date Assigned	Reading Assignment	Completion Date
	Chapters 1-4	
	Chapters 5-7	
	Chapters 8-10	
	Chapters 11-13	
	Chapters 14-16	
	Chapters 17-Epilogue	

UNIT OUTLINE - *The Devil's Arithmetic*

1	2	3	4	5
Library Writing Assignment #1	Work Session Nonfiction Rdg Assignment	Introduction PVR Ch 1-4	Study? Ch. 1-4 Writing Assignment #2	PVR Ch. 5-7 Oral Rdg Evaluation
6 Study ? Ch. 5-7 PV Ch. 8-10	**7** Read Ch. 8-10 (independently) Writing Conference	**8** Study ? Ch. 8-10 PVR Ch. 11-13	**9** Study ? Ch. 11-13 Vocabulary Reinforcement	**10** Figurative Language
11 PVR Ch. 14-16	**12** Study? Ch.14-16 Writing Assignment #3	**13** PVR Ch. 17-Epilogue	**14** Study ? Ch. 17-Epilogue Dramatization	**15** Speaker
16 Extra Discussion Questions/ Activities	**17** Extra Discussion Questions/ Activities	**18** Review	**19** Vocabulary Review	**20** Test

Key: P = Preview Study Questions   V = Vocabulary Work   R = Read

STUDY GUIDE QUESTIONS

SHORT ANSWER STUDY GUIDE QUESTIONS - *The Devil's Arithmetic*

Chapters 1-4

1. What is Hannah's complaint to her mother?
2. Where do Hannah and her family travel to get to her grandparents?
3. Why was Hannah's younger brother scared?
4. For whom is Hannah named?
5. What has Grandpa Will so upset?
6. When Hannah was younger what did she do that she thought would please her Grandpa Will?
7. Why does Aunt Eva light the candles in Grandma Belle's house every holiday?
8. Grandfather Will decides that Hannah is old enough to partake of what holiday tradition?
9. What part of the ceremony does Hannah's younger brother. Aaron, enjoy the most?
10. Why does the family open the door to admit the prophet Elijah?
11. What happens after Hannah goes to open the door and says, "Ready or not, here I come?"
12. On what does Hannah blame this daydream-like scene?
13. Where is Hannah and with whom?

Chapters 5-7

1. What does Shmuel admit to Hannah the next morning, the day of his wedding?
2. How do Gitl and Shmuel react to Hannah's ravings about her coming from New Rochelle, New York?
3. Who comes to visit them the morning of the wedding and what does he bring?
4. What does Gitl tell Hannah to wear to the wedding and how does Hannah feel about it?
5. Who does Hannah meet that she thinks will make her 'dream' experience more interesting?
6. Where does Hannah tell the girls she goes during the week that they find unbelievable?
7. Why were the shtetl girls especially fascinated with Hannah?
8. Why are the local girls shocked to hear Rachel's account of Shmuel and Fayge's courtship?
9. What quick observation does the badchan make of Hannah?
10. Why did Hannah laugh out loud after meeting the badchan?

Chapters 8-10

1. Why doesn't Fayge enjoy the "Sherele" wedding music and dance?
2. How does Fayge treat Hannah (Chaya) her soon-to-be-niece?
3. Tell what the wedding party sees upon gaining an open view of the village?
4. How does Hannah singularly figure out what is happening?
5. What does Hannah tell the rabbi to try to get him to turn back? What does he say?
6. In what manner did the intruders stop the procession from entering the synagogue?
7. What information do the Nazi officers give the group of villagers?
8. How does the rabbi try to calm the group?
9. How do the truckloads of Jews attempt to calm their fears on the way to resettlement?

10. What is the first thing the Jews notice upon their arrival at the train station?
11. After getting out of the trucks, what does the Nazi officer demand the villagers to do first?
12. Upon rising from lying on the ground, what are they made to do next?

Chapters 11-13

1. Describe the conditions of the boxcars and the length of time spent in them.
2. What message adorned the iron gates of the camp?
3. Why is Hannah made to surrender her blue hair ribbons?
4. What does the woman guard in the blue dress tell them to do first?
5. Why doesn't Hannah say anymore about what she remembers about the showers?
6. After her hair is shorn from her head, what does Hannah realize?
7. What command does Hannah impose upon herself to numb the shock?
8. After their heads are shaved and they survive the cold showers, where are they next sent?
9. What distressing information does the man who tattoos Hannah give her?
10. When Gitl leaves the barracks to find something to eat for the children, what is she told?
11. Why doesn't Gitl want Hannah to touch Tzipporah upon waking the next morning?
12. What instructions are the zugangi given pertaining to the bowls they are issued?
13. What message does the officer give to the newcomers after they have eaten?

Chapters 14-16

1. What does Rivka share with the girls about the rest of her family?
2. Rivka shares the rules she follows to stay alive at the camp one day at a time. What are they?
3. What does Hannah dream of the night Rivka tells them the rules of the camp?
4. What is the signal for the young children that the commandant is coming?
5. What job does Hannah have in the camp?
6. Where does Gitl work in the camp and what does she learn there?
7. Explain Rivka's definition of The Devil's Arithmetic.
8. Why does Hannah think that Reuven's choosing was her fault?
9. How does Rivka respond when Hannah suggests that they should at least go down fighting.
10. The night she finds out her father has been chosen, Fayge finally speaks to the girls. What is her story about?

Chapters 17-Epilogue
1. Why does Hannah come to expect that something out of the ordinary will soon happen?
2. What was the plan and who was included?
3. Was it successful?
4. How did Fayge react to Shmuel's impending punishment?
5. What did Hannah notice about the Kommandos that carried Fayge's body to Lilith's Cave?
6. In what way did Hannah find irony in the everyday events of nature surrounding the camp?
7. What was Hannah trying to tell the girls when the new guard confronted them?
8. What does the new guard tell them?
9. Which three girls does he choose?
10. How does Hannah change the course of events?
11. Explain what happens after Hannah takes Rivka's place with the other girls.
12. Where does Hannah find herself after the dark resolves itself?
13. After she sits down at the laden table with her family, at what does Hannah stare?
14. When Aunt Eva wants to explain it's meaning, how does Hannah surprise her?
15. What does Aunt Eva share with Hannah about her past when they were alone?
16. What does Emmanuel Ringelblum, Jewish historian, claim were the only victories of the camps?

STUDY GUIDE QUESTION ANSWERS - *The Devil's Arithmetic*

Chapters 1-4

1. What is Hannah's complaint to her mother?

   She doesn't want to go to the Seder dinner of Passover at her grandparents.

2. Where do Hannah and her family travel to get to her grandparents?

   They leave New Rochelle, New York and travel by car to the Bronx, New York City.

3. Why was Hannah's younger brother scared?

   He was to read the Four Questions from the Haggadah.

4. For whom is Hannah named?

   She is named for a dead friend of her favorite Aunt Eva's.

5. What has Grandpa Will so upset?

   He is watching a television newscast showing footage from the Holocaust.

6. When Hannah was younger what did she do that she thought would please her Grandpa Will?

   She took a ballpoint pen and wrote numbers on her arm to resemble his concentration camp tattoo.

7. Why does Aunt Eva light the candles in Grandma Belle's house every holiday?

   She had no house or family of her own and it is a privilege they extend to honor her.

8. Grandfather Will decides that Hannah is old enough to partake of what holiday tradition?

   She can now toast at the dinner table with wine.

9. What part of the ceremony does Hannah's younger brother. Aaron, enjoy the most?

   The snatching of and the hiding of the afikoman

10. Why does the family open the door to admit the prophet Elijah?

    It is a tradition to remind themselves of the time Jews were forced to keep their doors open to show the Christians they were not practicing blood rituals.

11. What happens after Hannah says, "Ready or not, here I come?"

    Hannah is transformed into another time and place.

12. On what does Hannah blame this daydream-like scene?

    She blames it on the wine she drank.

13. Where is Hannah and with whom?

     She is in a Polish shtetl with a pleasant man named Shmuel and his sister Gitl. Shmuel
     is to be married the next day. They call her Chaya (Hannah's Hebrew name), their niece,
     whom they have taken in after her parents' deaths. They speak in Yiddish, which
     Hannah is able to speak and understand perfectly.

Chapters 5-7

1. What does Shmuel admit to Hannah the next morning, the day of his wedding?

     He is afraid of *getting* married, but not *being* married to Fayge.

2. How do Gitl and Shmuel react to Hannah's ravings about her coming from New Rochelle,
   New York?

     They think her illness has affected her mentally. They are certain she is their niece,
     Chaya, from Lublin.

3. Who comes to visit them the morning of the wedding and what does he bring?

     Yitzchak, the red-headed butcher, and his two children come to help and he brings two
     cages of chickens for wedding presents.

4. What does Gitl tell Hannah to wear to the wedding and how does Hannah feel about it?

     She tells her to wear the blue sailor-suit dress she wore as a child to Shmuel's Bar
     Mitzvah. Hannah says it is a rag and feels it is suitable for a Halloween party.

5. Who does Hannah meet that she thinks will make her 'dream' experience more interesting?

     She meets a set of local girls her age, one of which is called Rachel. Rachel tells her she
     is going to be her best friend.

6. Where does Hannah tell the girls she goes during the week that they find unbelievable?

     She shares with them that she goes to school every week day. They say it is only for
     boys.

7. Why were the shtetl girls especially fascinated with Hannah?

     They loved her many stories of books she has read and movies she has seen.

8. Why are the local girls shocked to hear Rachel's account of Shmuel and Fayge's courtship?

     Fayge is marrying Shmuel for love. Most marriages there are arranged by the shadchan,
     the marriage broker.

9. What quick observation does the badchan make of Hannah?

     He calls her wise and an old girl in young-girl disguise.

10. Why did Hannah laugh out loud after meeting the badchan?

     She laughed at the idea of a Jewish jester, of which the badchan reminded her.

Chapters 8-10

1. Why doesn't Fayge enjoy the "Sherele" wedding music and dance?
   She says it is such a gloomy song for such a glorious event.

2. How does Fayge treat Hannah (Chaya) her soon-to-be-niece?
   She is very considerate and kind to her, offering her a ride and pleasant conversation.

3. Tell what the wedding party sees upon gaining an open view of the village?
   There are automobiles and trucks parked in front of the synagogue.

4. How does Hannah singularly figure out what is happening?
   She inquires of the date and makes the association from her memory of the history of the Holocaust.

5. What does Hannah tell the rabbi to try to get him to turn back?   How does he respond?
   She tells him that six million Jews will be killed by the Nazis and he says that it is only God before whom we must tremble.

6. In what manner did the intruders stop the procession from entering the synagogue?
   They joined together to make a perfect half circle in front of the synagogue doors.

7. What information do the Nazi officers give the group of villagers?
   They have already sent the rest of the village to resettlement and will be taking all of them now.

8. How does the rabbi try to calm the group?
   He restates the information given to him by the Nazis that the soldiers have promised to guard their village, stores, houses, and especially their synagogue while they are gone.

9. How do the truckloads of Jews attempt to calm their fears on the way to resettlement?
   They all loudly sing a song about a kidnapper who dragged men off to the army.

10. What is the first thing the Jews notice upon their arrival at the train station?
    They see baskets and bags belonging to their families spread out in piles along the train tracks.

11. After getting out of the trucks, what does the Nazi officer demand the villagers to do first?
    He orders them to lie down and when they do not move immediately, he fires his gun at their feet to get them to quickly follow his order.

12. Upon rising from lying on the ground, what are they made to do next?
    They are crammed into two boxcars and locked inside. Stories abound from the passengers of so-called rumors of atrocities committed against other Jews of which they have heard.

Chapters 11-13

1. Describe the conditions of the boxcars and the length of time spent in them.
    They were kept inside of them for four days and nights with one brief stop for each boxcar. It was like standing in an oven that smelled of human sweat, urine, and feces. Four dead bodies were slung out onto a siding and a dead baby was cast behind a horse watering trough.

2. What message adorned the iron gates of the camp?
    Work makes you free was written on the gates.

3. Why is Hannah made to surrender her blue hair ribbons?
    Hannah questions and speaks out to the woman guard. She is slapped on both cheeks.

4. What does the woman guard in the blue dress tell them to do first?
    She tells them to undress in order to go to the showers.

5. Why does Hannah decide not to say anymore about what she remembers about the Holocaust, especially the showers?
    She wants to be brave while waiting and not take away the others' hope, which is all they have.

6. After her hair is shorn from her head, what does Hannah realize?
    She has lost her memory. She'd been shorn of her memory as brutally as she'd been shorn of her hair, without permission, without reason. She is startled because all the girls and women look alike with no hair.

7. What command does Hannah impose upon herself to numb the shock?
    Don't think. Do.

8. After their heads are shaved and they survive the cold showers, where are they next sent?
    They are sent to a dimly lit room to find something to wear and then to be tattooed.

9. What distressing information does the man who tattoos Hannah give her?
    She is wearing his dead daughter's dress and Hannah's name is the same as hers, Chaya.

10. When Gitl tries to leave the barracks to find something to eat for the children, what does the young soldier tell her?
    He says, "they will get used to it." He then points to the smokestack saying, "That is Jew smoke. Learn to eat when it's given to you, Jew, or you, too, go up that stack."

11. Why doesn't Gitl want Hannah to touch Tzipporah upon waking the next morning?
   She has died in her sleep.

12. What instructions are the zugangi given pertaining to the bowls they are issued?
   Use them to wash, eat, and drink. Everything. The young girl, Rivka, handing them out calls them 'Every Bowls'.

13. What message does the officer give to the newcomers after they have eaten?
   You will work hard, never answer back, complain, or question or try to escape. All this will be done for the Fatherland.

Chapters 14-16
1. What does Rivka share with the girls about the rest of her family?
   During the year she has been in the camp, her mother, three sisters, father, and brother have all been sent to the ovens. Her remaining brother, Wolfe, must work as a Sonderkommando, one of the walking dead who handle the corpses.

2. Rivka shares the rules she follows to stay alive at the camp one day at a time. What are they?
   a. Learn to read prisoner's numbers. There are good numbers and bad numbers. Prisoners with numbers that begin with G(Greek) can't understand the German, and react too slowly. Stay away from them. b. Learn to organize. c. Never go through the door to Lilith's Cave. d. Help the little ones hide in the midden (the garbage dump) when the commandant comes. e. Do not ask why.

3. What does Hannah dream of the night Rivka tells them the rules of the camp?
   She dreams of a schoolyard where girls in blue dresses and blue pants hook arms and shut her out. She awakes crying, but does not remember of what she dreamed.

4. What is the signal for the young children that the commandant is coming?
   The older children and adults make a clucking noise by placing their tongues against the roof of their mouths.

5. What job does Hannah have in the camp?
   She and Shifre worked in the kitchen with Rivka: hauling water in large buckets, spooning out the meager meals, scrubbing the giant cauldrons, and scrubbing the walls and floors.

6. Where does Gitl work in the camp and what does she learn there?
   She works in the sorting shed, where the Jews' belongings are sorted. The men and women can talk there and find out the camp news.

7. Explain Rivka's definition of The Devil's Arithmetic.
> She shares that the cruel numbers of those processed and the rest of their remaining days add up or subtract to become the devil's arithmetic.

8. Why does Hannah think that Reuven's choosing was her fault?
> She thinks she should have told the commandant that he was her brother.

9. How does Rivka respond when Hannah suggests that they should at least go down fighting.
> She responds with , "It is harder to die this way than to go out shooting. We are all heroes here."

10. The night she finds out her father has been chosen, Fayge finally speaks to the girls. What is her story about?
> She tells a story of her father's about a young boy who removes Satan's heart, which is full of immeasurable pain, from a werewolf; and the earth swallows the black heart unto itself.

Chapters 17-Epilogue
1. How does Hannah come to expect that something out of the ordinary will soon happen?
> Gitl informs her that there is a plan and who is involved. She will not reveal what the plan is, but makes Chaya promise *to remember* if something happens to her and Shmuel because she is their only remaining flesh and blood.

2. What was the plan and who was included?
> It was a plan to escape from the camp one night. Gitl, Shmuel, Yitzchak, and Hannah were all part of it.

3. Was it successful?
> No, only Yitzchak escaped. Chaya and Gitl were able to reenter the barracks offering an excuse to the blokova. The six other men were caught that night, beaten, and the next morning shot in front of roll call.

4. How did Fayge react to Shmuel's impending punishment?
> She pushed through the crowd and flung herself at this feet. She was shot along with the men.

5. What did Hannah notice about the Kommandos that carried Fayge's body to Lilith's Cave?
> He carried her as one might carry a loved one, with tenderness and pride. Rivka informed them that he was her brother, Wolfe.

6. In what way did Hannah find irony in the everyday events of nature surrounding the camp?
> It was as if all nature ignored what went on in the camp. There were bright flowers, brilliant sunsets, and soft breezes. She thought that if this tragedy had been happening in a book, the skies would be weeping and the swallows mourning by the smokestack.

7. What was Hannah trying to tell the girls when the new guard confronted them?
   She was remembering history and parts of her former life. She was pleading with the girls to be certain to carry the message into the future to prevent what was happening there from ever happening again. They were perplexed with her talk and questioned her.

8. What does the new guard tell them?
   They need three more Jews to make a full load for the ovens. He was sent to find three of the commandant's pets that were not working. They were talking and not working.

9. Which three girls does he choose?
   He picks Esther, Shifre, and Rivka. Rivka asks Hannah, "Who will remember for you now?"

10. How does Hannah change the course of events?
    She removes the kerchief from Rivka's head, ties it hastily on hers, and takes her place with Esther and Shifre. She softly commands Rivka to "Run for her life, Run for her future, And to Remember.

11. Explain what happens after Hannah takes Rivka's place with the other girls.
    She puts her arms around their waists and begins to tell them a story about a girl from New Rochelle in America named Hannah Stern. Just as they all walk in the dark door of Lilith's Cave, Hannah says, " Ready or not here we come..."

12. Where does Hannah find herself after the dark resolves itself?
    She is back at her grandparents' open apartment door looking across an empty hall.

13. After she sits down at the laden table with her family, what does Hannah stare?
    She sits next to her favorite Aunt Eva staring at the tattooed number on her arm.

14. When Aunt Eva wants to explain it's meaning, how does Hannah surprise her?
    Hannah recognizes the number as Rivka's number and wants to explain what she has learned to her aunt. It is then that she realizes that (Aunt Eva) Rivka's brother, Wolfe, is her Grandpa Will.

15. What does Aunt Eva share with Hannah about her past when they were alone?
    She tells Hannah that of all the villagers Chaya had come to the camp with, only Gitl and Yitzchak survived. They both emigrated to Israel and remained close friends, until well into their seventies. Neither married and both thrived to bear witness.

16. What does Emmanuel Ringelblum, Jewish historian, claim were the only victories of the camps?
    He says that to resist being dehumanized and to witness and remember and outlive one's tormentors were the only victories.

MULTIPLE CHOICE FORMAT STUDY QUESTIONS

Chapters 1-4

1. What is Hannah's complaint to her mother?
    a. She wants to celebrate Easter with Rosemary.
    b. She can't find her best sweater to wear to the Seder.
    c. She wants to go with Rosemary to the movies.
    d. She doesn't want to go to the Seder dinner of Passover at her grandparents.

2. Where do Hannah's grandparents live?
    a. the Bronx
    b. Queens
    c. New Rochelle
    d. Trenton

3. Why was Hannah's younger brother scared?
    a. He never rode through New York City before that day.
    b. He was to read the Four Questions from the Haggadah.
    c. He never met all the relatives that were going to be at his house.
    d. He would be the first one to find the afikoman.

4. For whom is Hannah named?
    a. She is named for her favorite aunt.
    b. She is named for her grandmother.
    c. She is named for a dead friend of her favorite Aunt Eva's.
    d. She is named for her father's mother.

5. What has Grandpa Will so upset?
    a. He is watching a television newscast showing footage from the Holocaust.
    b. He is mad because everyone is late, as usual.
    c. He can't remember what his name was when he was in the death camp.
    d. He sees the commandant from the death camp on the TV.

6. When Hannah was younger what did she do that she thought would please her Grandpa Will?
    a. She memorized the Four Questions from the Haggadah.
    b. She took a ballpoint pen and wrote numbers on her arm.
    c. She baked him his favorite cake and it flopped.
    d. She crawled up in his lap and recited the Seder.

7. Why does Aunt Eva light the candles in Grandma Belle's house every holiday?
    a. She had no house or family of her own.
    b. It is a privilege Grandma Belle extends to honor her.
    c. It is their family tradition.
    d. All of the above

8. Grandfather Will decides that Hannah is old enough to
    a. partake of the wine toasting.
    b. open the door for Elijah.
    c. recite from memory the Four Questions.
    d. none of the above

9. Aaron mostly enjoys the
    a. hiding and the finding of the afikoman.
    b. opening of the door for Elijah.
    c. reading out of the Haggadah.
    d. feast that awaits the family at the table.

10. The Stern family opens the door to admit the prophet Elijah because
    a. it is a Jewish tradition.
    b. it reminds them of when Jews were forced to keep their doors open.
    c. it was to show the Christians they were not practicing blood rituals.
    d. all of the above

11. When Hannah says, "Ready or not, here I come,"
    a. her grandparents hug her tightly.
    b. she is impatient for the meal to begin.
    c. she is transformed into another time and place.
    d. none of the above

12. On what does Hannah blame the daydream-like scene?
    a. the wine
    b. her anger and impatience
    c. her aunt
    d. her imagination

13. Where is Hannah and with whom?
    a. She is in a Polish shtetl with a pleasant man named Shmuel and his sister Gitl.
    b. It is some place unfamiliar where they call her Chaya.
    c. A place where they speak Yiddish.
    d. all of the above

Chapters 5-7

1. Shmuel is frightened of being married.
    a. true
    b. false

2. When Hannah raves about living in New Rochelle Gitl and Shmuel
    a. think her illness has taken its toll on her.
    b. are ready to send her back to Lublin.
    c. want to take her back to Lublin to visit to be able to remember.
    d. regret having taken her in after her parents died.

3. Who comes to visit Shmuel and Gitl the morning of the wedding?
    a. Rabbi Boruch comes to call and brings with him the wedding ceremony book.
    b. Fayge, the bride, comes to be sure Shmuel is still willing to go through with it.
    c. Yitzchak, the red-headed butcher, and his two children come to help.
    d. none of the above

4. What does Gitl tell Hannah to wear to the wedding?
    a. She tells her to wear the blue sailor-suit dress she wore to Shmuel's Bar Mitzvah.
    b. A dress Hannah says is a rag.
    c. A dress Hannah thinks is suitable for a Halloween party.
    d. All of the above

5. Who does Hannah meet that she thinks will make her 'dream' experience more interesting?
    a. Rachel
    b. a group of four girls
    c. the butcher and his children
    d. the badchan

6. The shtetl girls wish they could go
    a. shopping on weekends.
    b. go to school like Hannah does.
    c. cut their hair like married girls.
    d. watch movies.

7. Hannah entertained the girls by
    a. reciting the Four Questions of Seder
    b. retelling movies and stories.
    c. singing songs from movies she'd seen.
    d. both a and b

8. Fayge and Shmuel's forthcoming marriage is the result of
    a. a mutual convenience.
    b. intense love.
    c. a shadchan's arrangement.
    d. money talks.

9. What quick observation does the badchan make of Hannah?
    a. He sees that she is dressed in a dress she doesn't like.
    b. He can tell she is different from the other girls.
    c. He looks into her eyes and sees the future.
    d. He calls her wise and an old girl in young -girl disguise.

10. What does the badchan remind Hannah of?
    a. a priest
    b. a fortuneteller
    c. a jester
    d. a clown

<u>Chapters 8-10</u>

1. Fayge is thrilled to do the wedding dance on the way to her village.
    a. false
    b. true

2. When Fayge meets Hannah she
    a. is jealous because Hannah has been able to spend time with Shmuel.
    b. treats her very consideration and kindness.
    c. asks her about her parents' death in Lublin.
    d. both b and c

3. When the wedding party approaches the village they see
    a. that the two lovebirds are wandering off to be alone.
    b. the rest of the village waiting for the ceremony.
    c. trucks and automobiles parked in front of the shul.
    d. that the synagogue is on fire.

4. Hannah is able to determine what is going to happen next because
    a. she can remember the history she has studied.
    b. the Nazi soldiers remind her of the TV program.
    c. she didn't really live there, she used to live in Lublin.
    d. she saw the Nazis in Lublin where they did the same thing to her village.

5. Hannah tells the rabbi
    a. to turn the wagons back.
    b. that six million Jews will die.
    c. not to ask her how she knows, she just does.
    d. all of the above

6. The officers allow the wedding party to progress into the shul and hold the service.
    a. true
    b. false

7. The officers tell the group that
    a. both c and d
    b. they are only following orders.
    c. they will guard their homes and stores while they are resettled.
    d. they have already taken the remaining villagers for resettlement.

8. To calm their fears, the Jews in the trucks
    a. knelt down and prayed.
    b. sang a kidnapping song loudly.
    c. both a and b
    d. none of the above

9. The first thing the group sees upon arrival at the train station is
    a. three empty boxcars.
    b. twenty Nazi-uniformed officers.
    c. their relatives' belongings placed in piles along the tracks.
    d. a crowd of neighboring Jews waiting for the train.

10. The Nazi officer demands that the group of Jews
    a. undress for a shower.
    b. both c and d
    c. hand over their papers and jewelry.
    d. lie down on the ground.

11. After the group has obeyed the officer's orders, they are
    a. herded into two boxcars and locked inside.
    b. sent back to their village, since the Nazis have their jewelry.
    c. told to wait for the next boxcars to be taken to their resettlement.
    d. asked what job skills they possess.

Chapters 11-13

1. Which of the following did not happen on the way to resettlement?
    a. Each boxcar was given two stops along the way.
    b. Stories were shared of other horrible treatment of Jews at the hands of Nazis.
    c. The boxcars smelled of human sweat, urine, and feces.
    d. Dead people and a baby were slung out of the boxcars like they were of no value.

2. What message adorns the gates of the camp?
    a. All work is done for the Fatherland.
    b. Work is good for you.
    c. All work and no play every day.
    d. Work will set you free.

3. Hannah speaks out and questions the woman guard so she
    a. is slapped on both cheeks.
    b. must surrender her blue hair ribbons.
    c. is denied her first meal.
    d. both a and b

4. After the group of women and girls undress for the shower, why doesn't Hannah share her memories?
    a. She is afraid of the blue-coated woman guard's temper.
    b. She wants to forget all the painful information she has stored.
    c. She wishes to allow the rest their hope, since it is all they have.
    d. All of the above.

5. After Hannah's hair has been shorn, she realizes
    a. she has lost her memory along with her hair.
    b. she cannot recall Gitl or Shmuel's name.
    c. she cannot find her friends, Rachel and Esther.
    d. both a and c

6. Choose the command Hannah gives herself to numb the shock.
    a. Do not look them in the eye.
    b. Dream and do as they say.
    c. Don't think. Do.
    d. One foot in front of the other.

7. Where were they sent immediately after their heads were shaved?
    a. to rummage through some piles of shoes
    b. to get some clothing from a dimly -lit room
    c. to get tattooed
    d. to get de-liced.

8. Select the one thing the man who tattooed Hannah did not tell her.
    a. He bought the dress in Lublin for his daughter, Chaya.
    b. She is wearing his daughter's dress.
    c. She has the same name as his daughter.
    d. She is the same age as his daughter.

9. When Gitl tries to leave the barracks to find something to eat for the children, what does the young soldier tell her?
    a. That is Jew smoke.
    b. Learn to eat when it's given to you.
    c. They will get used to it.
    d. All of the above.

10. When Hannah tries to brush the fly away from Tzipporah the next morning,
    a. she finds out that Tzipporah died in her sleep.
    b. Gitl turns away and cries.
    c. the barracks guard tells her to leave her alone.
    d. none of the above

11. Rivka tells the newcomers to use their Every Bowl for
    a. all of the below.
    b. washing.
    c. eating.
    d. drinking.

12. The Nazi commander tells the newcomers that they will
    a. never complain.
    b. be given small privileges.
    c. be given one attempt to escape.
    d. recite the Fatherland pledge daily at roll call.

Chapters 14-16

1. All of Rivka's family has been sent to the ovens since their arrival a year ago.
    a. true
    b. false

2. Select which rule Rivka says is the most important rule of survival in the camp.
    a. Help the little ones hide in the midden.
    b. Organize.
    c. Learn to read other prisoners' numbers.
    d. Do not ask why.

3. The night Rivka shares the rules for survival at camp Hannah dreams of
    a. the gas ovens and Lilith's cave.
    b. a schoolyard scene where she is an outcast.
    c. her Stern family in new Rochelle.
    d. a wonderful feast of roast beef and herbs.

4. The signal for the young children to hide in the midden when the commandant is coming is
    a. a clucking sound made by placing the tongue against the roof of the mouth.
    b. a sudden clapping of the hands twice.
    c. a ringing of the camp bell three times.
    d. none of the above

5. Hannah's camp job is to
    a. haul water in large buckets.
    b. spoon out the meager meals to the prisoners.
    c. scrub and walls, floors and cauldrons
    d. all of the above

6. What main advantage does Gitl's camp job afford her?
    a. She can bring things back to the barracks from the piles.
    b. She gets to know what prisoners are from where.
    c. She always knows when a new shipment of Jews has arrived.
    d. The men and women can talk in the sorting shed and news can be spread.

7. The Devil's Arithmetic is
    a. the number of new Jews that arrive every day at the camp.
    b. the adding and subtracting of the processed and those that are left; one more day alive.
    c. the difference between the amount of food served and the amount left to clean up.
    d. all of the above.

8. Hannah feels that Reuven's choosing was her fault because
    a. she should have warned him the officer was coming when he was on the hospital steps.
    b. she could have thrown herself over him to hide him.
    c. she didn't get him into the midden fast enough.
    d. she thinks she should have told the commandant he was her brother.

9. Rivka's response to Hannah's outrage that they should go down fighting is
    a. one of agreement.
    b. Both c and d
    c. We are all heroes here.
    d. It is harder to die this way than to go down fighting.

10. Fayge's story of the werewolf's heart full of pain is
    a. far above all the girls' understanding.
    b. meant to tell of the earth's wickedness and her pain at the loss of her father.
    c. is a strange tale to have been told by a rabbi.
    d. all of the above

Chapters 17-Epilogue

1. Select the one thing Hannah is not told by Gitl.
    a. You are our only flesh and blood, you must remember.
    b. The plan involves Yitzchak, Shmuel, me.
    c. I do not know the details.
    d. If I tell you, it could slip out.

2. Who was not included in the plan?
    a. Hannah
    b. Fayge
    c. Gitl
    d. Shmuel

3. Select the one prisoner who managed to escape according to the plan.
    a. Rabbi Reb Boruch
    b. Shmuel
    c. Gitl
    d. Yitzchak

4. Fayge was made to watch her beloved's execution.
    a. true
    b. false

5. Who is the Kommando carrying Fayge's body?
    a. He is Rivka's brother, Wolfe.
    b. He is just another one of the same cruel boys.
    c. He is boy form the village where Esther lived.
    d. He is a Nazi who wants to be an officer.

6. How did nature respond to the tragedies of the camp?
    a. There were brilliant sunsets.
    b. There were soft breezes.
    c. Bright flowers bloomed.
    d. All of the above

7. When the new guard confronted the girls they were
    a. listening to Hannah's ravings about the future.
    b. working hard, as usual.
    c. watching for commandant Breuer.
    d. clucking to warn the children to dive in the midden.

8. How many more bodies were needed to make a full load, according to the new guard?
   a. five
   b. two
   c. four
   d. three

9. Which of the following is not chosen?
   a. Esther
   b. Rivka
   c. Shifre
   d. Chaya

10. Whose place does Chaya secretly take?
   a. Esther's
   b. Rivka's
   c. Shifre's
   d. Rachel's

11. On the way to Lilith's Cave, Hannah begins to tell the girls a story about
   a. a girl named Cynthia from Israel.
   b. a U.S. Jewish president named Weisel.
   c. a girl named Hannah from New Rochelle.
   d. a girl named Rosemary from the Bronx.

12. Hannah finds herself back in her grandparents' apartment after she says,
   a. "her name was Rosemary and she had red hair."
   b. "Ready or not, here we come."
   c. "do not be afraid, we are all heroes here."
   d. " it is better than to go down fighting"

13. When Aunt Eva offers to explain her tattoo to Hannah, Hannah begins to sob.
   a. true
   b. false

14. Hannah learns from her Aunt Eva that
   a. Gitl dies in the camp.
   b. Grandpa Will was Wolfe, the Kommando who carried Fayge's body.
   c. Gitl and Yitzchak lived a long life in Israel.
   d. Both b and c

15. Emmanuel Ringelblum, Jewish historian, claims there were the victories of the camps.
   a. true
   b. false

ANSWER KEY- MULTIPLE CHOICE STUDY/QUIZ QUESTIONS
The Devil's Arithmetic

Chapters 1-4
1. D
2. A
3. B
4. C
5. A
6. B
7. D
8. A
9. A
10. D
11. C
12. A
13. D

Chapters 5-7
1. B
2. A
3. C
4. D
5. B
6. B
7. B
8. B
9. D
10. C

Chapters 8-10
1. A
2. B
3. C
4. A
5. D
6. B
7. A
8. B
9. C
10. B
11. A

Chapters 11-13
1. A
2. D
3. D
4. C
5. A
6. C
7. B
8. D
9. D
10. A
11. A
12. A

Chapters 14-16
1. B
2. C
3. B
4. A
5. D
6. D
7. B
8. D
9. B
10. B

Chapters 17- end
1. C
2. B
3. D
4. B
5. A
6. D
7. A
8. D
9. D
10. B
11. C
12. B
13. B
14. D
15. A

PREREADING VOCABULARY
WORKSHEETS

VOCABULARY - *The Devil's Arithmetic* Chapters 1-4

Part I: Using Prior Knowledge and Contextual Clues

Below are the sentences in which the vocabulary words appear in the text. Read the sentence. Use any clues you can find in the sentence combined with your prior knowledge, and write what you think the underlined words mean on the lines provided.

1. Her stomach felt heavy, as if the argument lay there like _unleavened_ bread.

_____

2. Hannah began a _gruesome_ tale about the walking dead, borrowing most of the characters, plot, and sound effects from a movie she'd seen on television the night before.

_____

3. For a moment, he stared at her _uncomprehendingly_.

_____

4., 5. She still occasionally dreamed of his _distorted_ face and the _guttural_ screams.

_____

_____

6. Although it was Grandma Belle's place to light the candles in her own home, over the years it had become a family tradition to let Aunt Eva do it, _compensation_ for not having a house or family of her own.

_____

7. Her grandfather droned on and on about the plagues and the _exodus_ from Egypt.

_____

8. Uncle Sam snorted and Aaron stopped, _mortified_.

_____

9. And she had discovered, with the very first toast, that she liked the sweet, _cloying_ taste of the wine, even though it made her head buzz.

_____

10. In a loud _conspiratorial_ whisper, Shmuel said, "She is waiting to hear from Avrom Morowitz, who went three years ago to America, promising to send for her."

_____

Devil's Arithmetic Vocabulary Worksheet Chapters 1-4 Continued

Part II: Determining the Meaning - Match the vocabulary words to their dictionary definitions. If there are words for which you cannot figure out the definition by contextual clues and by process of elimination, look them up in a dictionary.

____ 1. unleavened   A. secretly plotting
____ 2. gruesome   B. made without yeast
____ 3. uncomprehendingly   C. satisfying
____ 4. guttural   D. humiliated
____ 5. distorted   E. throaty; gravelly
____ 6. compensation   F. departure; exit
____ 7. exodus   G. benefits
____ 8. mortified   H. horrible
____ 9. cloying   I. deformed; twisted
____10. conspiratorial   J. without understanding

VOCABULARY - *The Devil's Arithmetic* Chapters 5-7

Part I: Using Prior Knowledge and Contextual Clues
   Below are the sentences in which the vocabulary words appear in the text. Read the sentence. Use any clues you can find in the sentence combined with your prior knowledge, and write what you think the underlined words mean on the lines provided.

1. She shivered, then followed him out to the barn, where they fed hay to the work horses, Popel and Hopel, in *companionable* silence.

_____

2. I will not have Fayge coming here and think me and all in this shtetl *slovens.*

_____

3. Sensing Hannah's *timidity*, Gitl kept her close as she greeted everyone by name, thanking them for the gifts as if she were the bride herself.

_____

4. "Chops off her hair!" *Appalled*, Shifre put her hands up to her own pale braids. "And not married?"

_____

5. She told the girls about *Yentl* and then about *Conan the Barbarian* with equal *vigor*.

_____

6. She told them the plot of *Little Women* in ten minutes, a miracle of *compression*, especially since her book report had been seven typed pages.

_____

7. She *mesmerized* them with her tellings.

_____

8. Walking through the woods behind the wagons, the girls kept *jostling* one another for the place of honor by Hannah's side.

_____

Devil's Arithmetic Vocabulary Worksheet Chapters 5-7 Continued

Part II: Determining the Meaning - Match the vocabulary words to their dictionary definitions. If there are words for which you cannot figure out the definition by contextual clues and by process of elimination, look them up in a dictionary.

_____ 1. companionable

_____ 2. slovens

_____ 3. timidity

_____ 4. appalled

_____ 5. vigor

_____ 6. compression

_____ 7. mesmerized

_____ 8. jostling

A. hypnotized; captivated

B. unclean; untidy

C. reduction

D. shyness

E. shocked

F. bouncing; bumping

G. energy

H. friendly; agreeable

VOCABULARY - *The Devil's Arithmetic* Chapters 8-10

Part I: Using Prior Knowledge and Contextual Clues - Below are the sentences in which the vocabulary words appear in the text. Read the sentence. Use any clues you can find in the sentence combined with your prior knowledge, and write what you think the underlined words mean on the lines provided.

1. She gave him a hug, and his normally *dour* face lit up.

_____

2. The medals on his chest caught the light from the spring sun, sending *undecipherable* signals across the market to them.

_____

3. "Sometimes she is *lucid* other times she talks of Rochelles and needles and snakes."

_____

4. They were a violent punctuation to all those *undistinguishable* sentences, as if Shmuel wanted to shake his fist in the Nazi's face but didn't dare.

_____

5. The government has *decreed* that we are to be relocated for the duration of this war.

_____

6. "At my request, the soldiers will pay special attention to the shul to make sure the peasants do not *desecrate* it."

_____

7. "But Reb Boruch, why would they *billet* soldiers here if they are needed elsewhere in the war?"

_____

8. She kept remembering more and more, about the death camps and the *crematoria*.

_____

9. There were armed guards standing in front of the station house door and scattered around the *periphery*.

_____

10. There was silence so *profound*, Hannah wondered if she had gone deaf.

_____

11. The proverbs say 'He who harps on a matter *alienates* his friend...'

_____

12. "Do not be *impudent*."

_____

Part II: Determining the Meaning - Match the vocabulary words to their dictionary definitions. If there are words for which you cannot figure out the definition by contextual clues and by process of elimination, look them up in a dictionary.

___ 1.	dour	A.	clear-headed
___ 2.	undecipherable	B.	unable to distinguish
___ 3.	lucid	C.	ruin; violate
___ 4.	undistinguishable	D.	heavy; penetrating
___ 5.	decreed	E.	sour; gloomy
___ 6.	desecrate	F.	furnace used for cremation
___ 7.	billet	G.	edge; fringe
___ 8.	crematoria	H.	cocky; arrogant
___ 9.	periphery	I.	distances
___ 10.	profound	J.	position
___ 11.	alienates	K.	unable to solve
___ 12.	impudent	L.	ordered

VOCABULARY - *The Devil's Arithmetic* Chapters 11-13

Part I: Using Prior Knowledge and Contextual Clues

Below are the sentences in which the vocabulary words appear in the text. Read the sentence. Use any clues you can find in the sentence combined with your prior knowledge, and write what you think the underlined words mean on the lines provided.

1. "No! said Hannah, surprised at the _vehemence_ in her response.

_____

2. Hannah thought they all looked so _vulnerable_, so helpless..

_____

3. He cut her hair without any _discernible_ skill, often pulling great clumps out with blunt scissors.

_____

4. Putting her hands on her hips, barely covering the _garish_ flowers on the red print dress, she smiled mockingly.

_____

5. In that dark, cold place it seemed like a kind of _affirmation_.

_____

6. And just when he had gotten it to the point of learning to eat nothing at all, the _ingrate_ up and died.

_____

7., 8. The smokestack and the _ominous_ black curl emerging from it, _dissipating_ against the bright sky, reminded her of something.

_____

_____

9. After the meal, the zugangi were lined up again in what seemed to Hannah to be a totally _arbitrary_ order, orchestrated by the same three-fingered woman.

_____

10. She dealt out slaps and pushes with such _fervor_ that they all did her bidding without protest.

_____

11. There--she had it, an _elusive_ slip of the memory.

_____

12. But the _raucous_ swallows, the woman's droning commands, the ground bass of the machinery mesmerized her.

_____

Part II: Determining the Meaning - Match the vocabulary words to their dictionary definitions. If there are words for which you cannot figure out the definition by contextual clues and by process of elimination, look them up in a dictionary.

___ 1. vehemence	A. loud; piercing
___ 2. vulnerable	B. puzzling; slippery
___ 3. discernible	C. erratic; inconsistent
___ 4. garish	D. passion; intensity
___ 5. affirmation	E. defenseless; exposed
___ 6. ingrate	F. approval
___ 7. ominous	G. threatening
___ 8. dissipation	H. ungrateful person
___ 9. arbitrary	I. tasteless; gaudy
___10. fervor	J. recognizable
___11. elusive	K. heated emotion
___12. raucous	L. disappearing

VOCABULARY - *The Devil's Arithmetic* Chapters 14-16

Part I: Using Prior Knowledge and Contextual Clues

    Below are the sentences in which the vocabulary words appear in the text. Read the sentence. Use any clues you can find in the sentence combined with your prior knowledge, and write what you think the underlined words mean on the lines provided.

1. Though she'd already gotten used to the *pervasive* camp smell, a cloudy musk that seemed to hang over everything, a mix of sweat and fear and sickness and the ever-present smoke that stained the sky, the smell in the midden was worse.

_____

2. She'd worried that the clothing would be *gaudy* signals to the commandant, but clearly he already knew.

_____

3. She and Shifre were set to work with Rivka in the kitchen hauling water in large buckets from the pump, spooning out *meager* meals, washing the giant cauldrons in which the soup cooked, scrubbing the walls and floors.

_____

4. Those big blue eyes and the *luminous*, infrequent smiles reminded her of someone she couldn't name.

_____

5. The commandant was a small, handsome man, so clean-shaven his face seemed *burnished*.

_____

6. Gitl began reciting the Kaddish, rocking back and forth on the sleeping shelf with the *sonorous* words, and the prayer was like the tolling of a death bell.

_____

7. But before Rivka could answer, a shout from the gate end of the compound *riveted* them.

_____

8. It moved *relentlessly* toward the hospital, which squatted at the compound's end.

_____

Devil's Arithmetic Vocabulary Worksheet Chapters 14-16 Continued

Part II: Determining the Meaning - Match the vocabulary words to their dictionary definitions. If there are words for which you cannot figure out the definition by contextual clues and by process of elimination, look them up in a dictionary.

____ 1. pervasive		A. showy
____ 2. gaudy		B. skimpy
____ 3. meager_		C. polished; waxed
____ 4. luminous		D. caught attention
____ 5. burnished		E. steadily; constantly
____ 6. sonorous		F. widespread
____ 7. riveted		G. deep, full sound
____ 8. relentlessly		H. bright; shining

VOCABULARY - *The Devil's Arithmetic* Chapters 17-Epilogue

Part I: Using Prior Knowledge and Contextual Clues
Below are the sentences in which the vocabulary words appear in the text. Read the sentence. Use any clues you can find in the sentence combined with your prior knowledge, and write what you think the underlined words mean on the lines provided.

1. There had been no signs or *portents*, no secret signals.

_____

2. And then there came a shout. A shot. And another. And another, rumbling *staccato*.

_____

3. Her mouth twisted at the *irony* of it and she turned to the three girls at the water pump.

_____

4. Suddenly, with great clarity, she saw another scene *superimposed* upon it: two laughing girls at a water fountain.

_____

5., 6. All the facts about the horrible *routinization* of evil in the camps is true: the nightmare journeys in the cattle cars, the shaving of heads, the choosing of victims for *incineration*.

_____

_____

7. The unnamed camp I have written about did not exist. Rather, it was an *amalgam* of the camps that did.

_____

8. Even with the facts in front of us, the numbers, the *indelible* photographs, the autobiographies, the wrists still bearing the long numbers, there are people in the world who deny such things actually happened.

_____

9. There is no way that fiction can come close to touching how truly inhuman, alien, even *satanic*, was the efficient machinery of death at the camps.

_____

10. That heroism- to resist being *dehumanized*, to simply outlive one's tormentors, to practice the quiet, everyday caring for one's equally tormented neighbors.

_____

Part II: Determining the Meaning - Match the vocabulary words to their dictionary definitions. If there are words for which you cannot figure out the definition by contextual clues and by process of elimination, look them up in a dictionary.

___ 1. portents	A. contradiction
___ 2. staccato	B. burning
___ 3. irony	C. put into a system
___ 4. superimposed	D. mixture; combination
___ 5. incineration	E. deprived of human dignity
___ 6. routinization	F. unforgettable; permanent
___ 7. amalgam	G. of Satan
___ 8. indelible	H. loud, abrupt sounds
___ 9. satanic	I. indication; omens
___10. dehumanized	J. one image on top of another

ANSWER KEY - VOCABULARY
The Devil's Arithmetic

Chapters 1-4
1. B
2. H
3. J
4. E
5. I
6. G
7. F
8. D
9. C
10. A

Chapters 5-7
1. H
2. B
3. D
4. E
5. G
6. C
7. A
8. F

Chapters 8-10
1. E
2. K
3. A
4. B
5. L
6. C
7. J
8. F
9. G
10. D
11. I
12. H

Chapters 11-13
1. D
2. E
3. J
4. I
5. F
6. H
7. G
8. L
9. C
10. K
11. B
12. A

Chapters 14-16
1. F
2. A
3. B
4. H
5. C
6. G
7. D
8. E

Chapters 17- Epilogue
1. I
2. H
3. A
4. J
5. B
6. C
7. D
8. F
9. G
10. E

DAILY LESSONS

LESSON ONE

Objectives

1. To give students background information for *The Devil's Arithmetic*
2. To give students the opportunity to fulfill their nonfiction reading assignment that goes along with this unit
3. To give students practice using library resources
4. To prepare students for the introductory activity in Lesson Two.
5. To give students the opportunity to write to inform by developing and organizing facts to convey information.

Activity

Assign one of each of the following topics to each of your students. Distribute Writing Assignment #1. Discuss the directions in detail. Take your students to the library so they may work on the assignment. Students should fill out a "Nonfiction Assignment Sheet" for at least one of the sources they used, and students should submit these sheets with their compositions.

1. List the basic beliefs of the Jewish religion.
2. Define anti-Semitism.
3. What was the Holocaust?
4. List the Jewish holidays and how they are celebrated.
5. Discover what is meant by the term bear witness, especially in reference to the Holocaust.
6. Create a list of known Holocaust survivors that have gone on to 'bear witness' in a public or private way.
7. Write a short biography of Adolf Hitler.
8. Explain what a Nazi was.
9. Make a timeline of World War II.
10. Who were the Allies and name their leaders.
11. Name the Axis countries and their leaders.
12. What was a concentration camp?
13. Where were concentration camps located?
14. What was a Jewish ghetto?
15. Identify European countries' boundaries in 1943. Compare to present boundaries.
16. Discover what countries remained neutral during World War II and why.
17. Explain the significance of the Star of David symbol.
18. What is a synagogue and a rabbi?
19. What was Hitler's Final Solution?
20. Locate Poland on a map and list its surrounding European neighbors.
21. Locate the Bronx, New York City, and New Rochelle, New York.
22. Use a Yiddish dictionary to define the following: goy, goyish, shul, shmattes, shadchan, klezmer, blokova, malach ha-mavis, badchan, rendar, mishigaas, schnorrers, schnell, afikoman, dayenu, drek, musselman, zugangi, sonderkommando, shtetl, yarmulkes

WRITING ASSIGNMENT #1 - *The Devil's Arithmetic*

PROMPT

You are going to read about a modern twelve-year-old girl who time travels to a Polish village during the 1940's era to experience first-hand what her family has been through. It is realistic or historical fiction (the events in the novel *could* have taken place, but the characters and events are *fictional*). Before you read it, however, you should have some background information about some of the things mentioned in the story.

You have been assigned one topic about which you must find information. You are to read as much as you can about that topic and write a composition in which you relate what you have learned from your reading. Note that this is a *composition*, not just a sentence or two.

PREWRITING

You will go to the library. When you get there, use the library's resources to find information about your topic. Look for books, encyclopedias, articles in magazines- anything that will give you the information you require. Take a few notes as you read to help you remember important dates, names, places, or other details that will be important in your composition.

After you have gathered information and become well-read on the subject of your report, make a little outline, putting your facts in order.

DRAFTING

You will need an introductory paragraph in which you introduce your topic.

In the body of your composition, put the "meat" of your research- the facts you found- in paragraph form. Each paragraph should have a topic sentence (a sentence letting the reader know what the paragraph will be about) followed by an explanation, examples or details.

Write a concluding paragraph in which you summarize the information you found and conclude your report.

PROMPT

After you have finished a rough draft of your paper, revise it yourself until you are happy with your work. Then, ask a student who sits near you to tell you what he/she likes best about your work, and what things he/she thinks can be improved. Take another look at your composition, keeping in mind your critic's suggestions, and make the revisions you feel are necessary.

PROOFREADING

Do a final proofreading of your paper double-checking your grammar, spelling, organization, and the clarity of your ideas.

NONFICTION ASSIGNMENT SHEET
(To be completed after reading the required nonfiction article)

Name _____ Date _____

Title of Nonfiction Read _____

Written By _____ Publication Date _____

I. Factual Summary: Write a short summary of the piece you read.

II. Vocabulary
    1. With which vocabulary words in the piece did you encounter some degree of difficulty?

    2. How did you resolve your lack of understanding with these words?

III. Interpretation: What was the main point the author wanted you to get from reading his work?

IV. Criticism
    1. With which points of the piece did you agree or find easy to accept? Why?

    2. With which points of the piece did you disagree or find difficult to believe? Why?

V. Personal Response: What do you think about this piece? OR How does this piece influence your ideas?

LESSON TWO

<u>Objectives</u>
1. To further allow students the opportunity to complete lengthy assignment given in Lesson One.
2. To provide students with the time to share their Nonfiction Reading Assignments

<u>Activity # 1</u>
Assist students with appropriate research as outlined in Lesson One.

<u>Activity # 2</u>
Ask students to share the results of their Nonfiction Reading Assignment Sheets with the group. Either in pairs, small groups, or in front of the whole class as time permits.

LESSON THREE

<u>Objectives</u>
1. To introduce *The Devil's Arithmetic* unit
2. To distribute books and other related materials (study guides, reading assignments, etc.)
3. To check students' nonfiction reading assignments
4. To model effective oral reading skills by reading aloud pages 3-7
5. To have students identify setting and point of view

Note: Prior to this class period, you need to have put up a bulletin board titled: A Time to Remember. Be sure to have a world map, or one of Europe and of the United States posted. If you do not have a bulletin board to use, use a big sheet of paper put over the chalkboard or a flip-chart style paper on an easel.

<u>Activity #1</u>
Provide students with a plain file card, posterboard strip, or something similar. Have each of them write one fact he/she learned from his/her research. Students could briefly illustrate their fact card, if time allows. Have students one by one, bring their fact up to the bulletin board and post it. Encourage placement for an attractive display. Students could also write directly on the bulletin board paper. After they have placed their fact up, have them share what they learned from their research. Discuss each fact briefly as it is presented so all students will be exposed to a wide variety of background information before reading.

TRANSITION: After all students have had the opportunity to share, ask students what they think it would have been like to live in a Nazi -occupied Polish village in Europe during World War II, especially if they were Jewish? Next ask them, how would their lives have been affected if they

WRITING ASSIGNMENT #2 - *The Devil's Arithmetic*

PROMPT

You have begun to read a story about a young Jewish girl who is struggling with her family's traditions and history. Through the course of the novel, Hannah develops into an altogether different character than she appears in the first four chapters. The author's technique of using time travel to grant Hannah the first-hand experience of what her family has endured is quite worthy of your comment.

Your assignment is to keep a diary during the time we are reading this novel. Each entry must be at least ten to fifteen sentences long. You may make your entries longer if you wish. You must have at least one entry for each reading assignment. (A total of six entries is the minimum requirement.)

PREWRITING

What will you write about? After your reading assignment has been completed, go back and review the events in it. Respond to Hannah's thoughts, experiences, and actions. React to the vivid descriptions of this totally foreign environment. What would you have done if you would have been Hannah? Would you have done things differently? In what ways? How would you have felt in her situation? What have you learned about her religion or family? Her instincts? Her personality? Her intelligence? Her values? Include anything else you find worthy of comment. I think there will be quite a bit that you'll find merits your review.

DRAFTING

What is important is that you sit down and write after each reading assignment or even more frequently. Diaries are not formal, written papers; they are a form of personal expression. There is no right or wrong thing to include in your diary. There is no formal structure- just take the time to get comfortable and let the ideas flow.

PROOFREADING

It can be quite a self-revealing exercise to go back and reread your earlier entries- not so much for proofreading purposes but to re-evaluate yourself and your feelings. One of the best ways to get to know yourself is to keep a diary or journal. We are all too frequently rushing here and there, with fleeting thoughts coming and going like wisps of smoke. It can be very helpful to slow down at some point, and record your thoughts and feelings for the day. Hopefully, this will not be the last diary you will ever write.

LESSON FIVE

Objectives
    1. To preview the study questions for chapters 5-7
    2. To familiarize students with the vocabulary for chapters 5-7
    3. To read chapters 5-7 in class
    4. To give students practice reading orally
    5. To evaluate students' oral reading

Activity #1
    Give students about ten minutes to preview the study questions for Chapters 5-7 and to do the related vocabulary work.

Activity #2
    Have students read Chapters 5-7 orally in class. You probably know the best way to get readers within your class; pick students at random, ask for volunteers, have students who have just read select another student, assign numbers to students and spin a spinner, or whatever works best for you. Complete the oral reading evaluation form that follows this lesson after listening to your students read. If students do not complete reading Chapters 5-7 in class, they should do so prior to the next class meeting____

ORAL READING EVALUATION

Name _____ Class____ Date _____

SKILL	EXCELLENT	GOOD	AVERAGE	FAIR	POOR
Fluency	5	4	3	2	1
Clarity	5	4	3	2	1
Audibility	5	4	3	2	1
Pronunciation	5	4	3	2	1
_____	5	4	3	2	1
_____	5	4	3	2	1

Total _____   Grade _____

Comments:

<u>LESSON SIX</u>

<u>Objectives</u>
      1. To review the main events and ideas of chapters 5-7
      2. To preview the study questions and vocabulary for chapters 8-10

<u>Activity #1</u>
      Hand out four little slips of paper or mini cards to each student that have the letters A,B,C, or D on them. A good idea is to use different color cards for each letter. Use the multiple choice study guide questions and answers on Chapters 5-7 for an oral review. Read the question (and/ or show it on the overhead). Then give students the four possible answers, labeling them A, B, C, or D (or show on overhead again). Students respond by holding up the card with what they think is the correct answer. This is one variety of Every Student Response. Remind students not to look at what others are holding up, but to simply display the card of their choice. This is a quick indicator of students' comprehension. You can make it somewhat different by requiring complete silence and having them read the questions silently from the overhead, or make it more mysterious (fun?) by blindfolding everyone and have them hold up a certain number of fingers per answer instead of using the cards.

<u>Activity #2</u>
      Have students independently preview chapters 8-10 vocabulary and study questions. If there is remaining time, have them work on their personal journal entries for the second set (Ch. 5-7) of reading.

<u>LESSON SEVEN</u>

<u>Objectives</u>
      1. To independently read chapters 8-10
      2. To evaluate students' writing
      3. To have students revise their Writing Assignment #1 papers

<u>Activity #1</u>
      Have students read chapters 8-10 silently in class while you meet with students individually for their writing conferences.

<u>Activity #2</u>
      Call students to your desk (or some other private area) to discuss their papers from Writing Assignment #1. Use the following Writing Evaluation Form to help structure your conference. Give students a date when their revisions are due.

WRITING EVALUATION FORM - *The Devil's Arithmetic*

Name _____ Date _____

Writing Assignment #1 for *The Devil's Arithmetic* unit   Grade _____

Circle One For Each Item:

Description (paragraph 1)	excellent	good	fair	poor
Plans (body paragraphs)	excellent	workable	fair	not realistic
Conclusion	excellent	good	fair	poor
Grammar:	excellent	good	fair	poor (errors noted)
Spelling:	excellent	good	fair	poor (errors noted)
Punctuation:	excellent	good	fair	poor (errors noted)
Legibility:	excellent	good	fair	poor

Strengths:

Weaknesses:

Comments/Suggestions:

LESSON EIGHT

<u>Objectives</u>
1. To review the vocabulary and main events and ideas from chapters 8-10
2. To preview the study questions and vocabulary for chapters 11-13
3. To practice making predictions

<u>Activity #1</u>

Use the multiple choice format of the study guide questions for chapters 8-10 as a quiz to check that students have done the required reading and to review the main ideas of chapters 8-10. Exchange papers for checking. Discuss answers and make sure students take notes for studying purposes.

<u>Activity #2</u>

Have students pair up and look over study guide questions for chapters 11-13. After they look over them, tell them to write down what they predict will be the answers to the questions. Have each partner predict half of the answers. Ask them to jot down their answers on a single piece of paper and put away temporarily. Discuss *why* as a whole group they made the prediction that they did for each of the questions, if time allows.

<u>Activity #3</u>

Have students spend about 10 minutes completing the prereading vocabulary page for chapters 11-13. After they have done that, pair them up. Have one member of each pair "act" out one of the words, while the other one tries to guess the word. Do this until all of the vocabulary words have been covered at least once. Students could be in small groups, as well. This is similar to the game Charades.

LESSON NINE

<u>Objectives</u>
1. To review main events and ideas in chapters 11-13
2. To review and practice previous vocabulary

<u>Activity</u>

Divide the class into two teams. Play a game like a spelling bee, but instead of spelling a word, they must answer one of the study questions correctly. Using the study guide questions for chapters 11-13, begin play. 1. Determine which team goes first. 2. Read one of the questions for one team member to answer. 3. If it was answered correctly, that team gets a point. 4. If it was not answered correctly, the other team gets a try at the same question. 5. Question goes back and forth until it is answered correctly. 6. Read another question, and repeat earlier play. 7. Continue until all questions for chapters 12-15 have been answered correctly. 8. Reward winning team with some small prize or other incentive.

Continue the game substituting vocabulary and their definitions from earlier chapters for the study guide question and its answer.

66

LESSON TEN

Objectives
1. To introduce simile and metaphor as figures of speech
2. To have students locate figurative language in the text
3. To create original figures of speech
4. To illustrate figurative language

Activity #1

Tell the class you are going to read a few sentences to them from their most recently read chapters in the book. Ask them to listen carefully and try to identify similarities between them or see if they can identify what they are examples of:

▾   Everything felt strange, alien, as if she were on another planet, as if she were on the moon.
▾   Her long black hair was like a blanket over her.
▾   Part of the moon still hung in the sky, a pale halo over his blond head.
▾   Hannah felt hope, like a small bubble rise from her empty stomach.
▾   The silence was like a prayer.
▾   It was like standing in an oven.

Activity #2

Make two columns on the chalkboard labeling each one separately: simile and metaphor. Spend some time here instructing about these two forms of figurative language that illustrate comparisons. You could use specific examples from the following test, focusing on the ones from earlier chapters. Perhaps you could cite some examples from familiar songs. Ask why they think any author or lyricist would use them? Do they use them? Why? In what way does using them enhance speaking or writing or the understanding of each of these. As a whole group, have students give you examples they can think of and then have them locate a few in any part of the text they have read. Allow them to come to the board and write these under the correct heading. When you are satisfied with their ability to recognize them and differentiate between them, go to the next activity.

Activity #3

Divide the class into small groups of three or four. Have each group assign a recorder. Give them a couple of sheets of paper. Ask each group to locate as many of these figures of speech as they can from the text. They may be more successful in the portion they already have read, but it isn't necessary to limit them. Giving them a time constraint is an option. It could be a race, you are the judge. You may want to rule out using the ones that are posted on the board. It's up to you. Wrap this activity up by having the group with the **most** read their list aloud. Decide as a whole group if indeed each one is correct. Have all groups check off the ones that are read that they also found. Allow every group to read any that have not yet been mentioned. You could give small treats for first, second, third place, etc.

67

<u>Activity #4</u>
Have students create one example of each type. They could be individual sentences or you could require them to write a short paragraph using both. Base this on the ability level of your students and/or time. Create one together as a model. If time, have them illustrate it with original art work or magazine pictures. Save finished products for display. They could do this part as homework.

NOTE: The following figurative language test is optional. You may want to use it right after instruction, later in this unit, or not at all. You may choose to use it only as a resource for this lesson. It contains examples from the entire book.

FIGURATIVE LANGUAGE TEST - *Devil's Arithmetic*

I. Read the following examples of figurative language. Label each one separately with either an **S** for simile, or an **M** for metaphor. **BONUS**: Locate the two that are another type of figurative language: personification (inanimate objects take on animate qualities).

1. And the irony of it was that he was as gentle as a lamb.
2. The talk and laughter at the table dipped and soared about them like swallows.
3. Hannah slipped into the chair knowing it was the one the family reserved for the prophet Elijah, who slipped through the centuries like a fish through water.
4. She forced herself to come back into focus; it was like turning a camera lens.
5. The sky is our canopy.
6. Birds cried out merrily from the woods and the tops of the trees danced to the rhythms all their own.
7. Above them in the cloudless sky, stars were scattered as thick as sand.
8. The nameless zugangi were shipped along the rails of death.
9. The earth opened and swallowed the black heart into itself.
10. You want to be a hero, like Joshua at Jericho, like Samson against the Philistines.
11. She felt a sudden coldness strike through her as if an ice dagger had been plunged into her belly.
12. The prayer was like the tolling of a death bell.
13. The children dropped their clothes like bright rags on the sandy ground.
14. From all over the camp came the same clicking, as if crazed crickets had invaded the place.
15. It was like a waterfall of information.
16. She lay there curled in a ball, her finger in her mouth like a stopper in a bottle.
17. The women and the children lay as still as corpses.
18. Part of the moon still hung in the sky, a pale halo over his blond head.
19. At sixteen I was a giant!
20. He stood up slowly, unfolding like some kind of long-legged bird.

II. List one example of your own for each type of figurative language. They can be original or from your favorite songs or poetry.

III. Illustrate your favorite example of figurative language from those listed.

ANSWER KEY- FIGURATIVE LANGUAGE TEST - *Devil's Arithmetic*

I.

1. S
2. S
3. S
4. S
5. M
6. P
7. S
8. M
9. P
10. S
11. S
12. S
13. S
14. S
15. S
16. S
17. S
18. M
19. M
20. S

II. Answers will vary.

III. Creative response.

LESSON ELEVEN

Objectives

    1. To check earlier predictions from chapters 11-13
    2. Preview vocabulary and main events from chapters 14-16
    3. To read orally in class chapters 14-16

Activity #1

Have students retrieve their earlier predictions and now check for accuracy. Award with a small incentive those with a high percentage of correct answers.

Activity #2

Have students complete the prereading vocabulary work independently for chapters 14-16. Pass out plain paper for drawing, or use individual easels or slates. Have students select a partner for this activity. Have one of the partners sketch their impression of one of the vocabulary words within a limited amount of time. The other one is to guess which vocabulary word he/she is trying to picture. When the correct word has been chosen, play turns to the other partner. Continue play until all vocabulary words have been covered. This is similar to the game Pictionary. It could also be done in small groups.

Activity #4

Quickly have students skim the study guide questions for these chapters, setting the purpose for reading. Read chapters 14-16 in class. Have a session of "spirit reading" when any student can pick up reading (when the spirit moves them) uninvited or unannounced, at the beginning of any new paragraph or page. (This helps eliminate those who will break in on someone after only one sentence or a couple of words is read) Guidelines need to be set also such as: everyone in the class must read at least once, but otherwise participation is unlimited. Try to stop and have class recap often because students can get caught up in the 'spirit of things' and pay more attention to who has and hasn't read than the content of the material.

LESSON TWELVE

<u>Objective</u>
1. To review the main ideas and events from chapters 14-16
2. To give students practice in writing to persuade

<u>Activity #1</u>
Use the multiple choice format of the study guide questions for Chapters 14-16 as a quiz to check students' comprehension of these pages and to review the main ideas and events of these chapters. Exchange papers for grading. Discuss answers and make sure students take notes for studying purposes.

<u>Activity #2</u>
Distribute Writing Assignment #3 and discuss directions in detail. In the remaining class time, have students begin work on this assignment. Be sure to give students specifics on when assignment is due.

WRITING ASSIGNMENT #3 - *The Devil's Arithmetic*

PROMPT

Since you have finished reading chapter 16, you know that Yitzchak's small son, Reuven, is chosen by the commandant. The commandant makes a cruel joke of this small, defenseless child. Hannah is overwhelmed that she didn't act differently in order to save this innocent little boy.

In this writing assignment, you are to pretend you are Hannah, at the camp when the commandant drives up and sees Reuven coming out of the hospital. Your objective is to convince the Nazi commandant that this blameless and motherless child need not be chosen to go with him.

PREWRITING

To begin with, list any and all possible arguments you can think that you could use in this instance. Decide which are your strongest justifiable arguments, and which are less substantial. Organize your points from weaker to strongest and jot down anything you can think of which will support or explain your arguments.

DRAFTING

Begin with an introductory paragraph in which you express your intent to take responsibility for and look after Reuven for the reminder of his life. Follow that with one paragraph for each of the main points you have to support your argument to convince Breuer to release Reuven to your care. Fill in each paragraph with reasons and feelings that support your main point. Then, write an ending paragraph that summarizes your commitment to Reuven's well-being and your continued service to the commandant's wishes and the Fatherland as your final statement.

PROMPT

When you finish the rough draft of your paper, ask a student who sits near you to read it. After reading your rough draft, he\she should tell you what he\she liked best about your work, which parts were difficult to understand, and ways in which your work could be improved. Reread your paper considering your critic's comments, and make the corrections you think are necessary.

PROOFREADING

Do a final proofreading of your paper double-checking your grammar, spelling, organization, and the clarity of your ideas.

LESSON THIRTEEN

Objectives
1. To preview the study guide questions for chapters 17-Epilogue
2. To do the prereading vocabulary work for chapters 17- Epilogue
3. To read these chapters orally in class with a partner

Activity #1
   Give students copies of the short answer quiz for chapters 17- Epilogue. Have them skim through the questions to form some ideas about how the book will end.

Activity # 2
   Have students glance over the vocabulary from chapters 17-Epilogue. Write each of the words on the chalkboard, leaving space beneath each one. Divide the class into ten teams or pairs. Have each team list as many synonyms for their word as they can come up with, beneath it, on the chalkboard. Give them a time limit and reward the team who comes up with the most correct synonyms. It is up to you if you want them to be able to refer to a thesaurus or dictionary first.

Activity #3
   Allow students to choose a partner with which to partner-read these chapters quietly. Each partner should read the same amount of text.

LESSON FOURTEEN

Objectives
1. To review the vocabulary and main events and ideas from Chapters 17-Epilogue
2. To encourage students to recreate and interpret scenes from their reading
3. To reinforce the true aspects of this novel

Activity #1
   Make a copy of the study guide questions with answers and the matching vocabulary section from Chapters 17- Epilogue. Cut them apart, separating the questions and answers or vocabulary word and definition into two piles. Divide the class into two teams. Give one team the questions (or vocab word) ; the other team the answers (or definition). Divide them up among the players so only one person has one question or answer. Select one team to begin play. One person from that team reads one of the questions or answers. Next, a member from the other team tries to match up with the corresponding response. When it is a correct match, move on to another question. Continue play until all questions are answered correctly.

<u>Activity #2</u>

Allow students to select a favorite portion of the text and "act" it out briefly using the books. Stress that this is a 'just for fun 'session and encourage those uncomfortable with acting to provide sound effects or narration.

<u>Activity #3</u>

Reread the Epilogue together orally. Thoughtfully discuss the author's use of research and how she was able to weave these elements into this story.

<u>LESSON FIFTEEN</u>

<u>Objectives:</u>
1. To make available a real-life resource on the Holocaust
2. To compose thank you notes

<u>Activity #1</u>

In preparation for this lesson, have students prepare a list of questions about the Holocaust that was not answered through the reading of this book. Ask them to review the book for ideas or points of horror, interest, or curiosity. This could be part of your extra discussion/activities classes.

<u>Activity #2</u>

Contact a local Jewish synagogue or agency that is willing to provide a speaker. Set the date up with the agency based on your timetable. If at all possible, allow the guest to preview *The Devil's Arithmetic* or summarize for him/her prior to his visit. In this way, the speaker will know from what frame of reference the class, as an audience, is coming,

<u>Activity #3</u>

Have speaker address class on the Holocaust. Perhaps instances of bearing witness could be shared that have led to healing. The content of the message will be contingent upon the experience of the speaker, if it is an actual survivor, or another Jewish authority.

<u>Activity #4</u>

After the speaker has finished, briefly review components of writing a *thank you* note. Assign these for homework. Perhaps you could generate a creative piece of stationery for students to utilize. Mail to speaker

LESSONS SIXTEEN AND SEVENTEEN

Objectives
    1. To discuss the ideas and themes from The Devil's Arithmetic in greater detail
    2. To have students exercise their interpretive and critical thinking skills
    3. To try to relate some of the ideas in *The Devil's Arithmetic* to the students' lives

Activity #1
    Choose the questions from the Extra Discussion Questions/Writing Assignments which seem most appropriate for your students. A class discussion of these questions is most effective if students have been given the opportunity to formulate answers to the questions prior to the discussion. To this end, you may either have all the students formulate answers to all the questions, divide your class into groups and assign one or more questions to each group, or you could assign one question to each student in your class. The option you choose will make a difference in the amount of class time needed for this activity.

Activity #2
    After students have had ample time to formulate answers to the questions, begin your class discussion of the questions and the ideas presented by the questions. Be sure students take notes during the discussion so they have information to study for the unit test.

EXTRA DISCUSSION QUESTIONS/WRITING ASSIGNMENTS
The Devil's Arithmetic

<u>Interpretive</u>

1. From what point of view is the story written? How would the story have been different if told from another perspective?

2. Identify the setting and tell how it dictates this story.

3. What are the main conflicts in the story and how are they resolved?

4. What is foreshadowing? Give some examples of the many instances of foreshadowing used in *The Devil's Arithmetic*.

5. Based on the facts in the story, can you determine the year and month most of this story takes place? Over what amount of time does the entire story span from beginning to end?

6. Give a complete character analysis of Hannah/Chaya.

7. Analyze the qualities and character traits of these characters: Mrs. Stern, Grandpa Will, Aunt Eva, Gitl, Shmuel, and Rivka. How do the roles they play differ?

8. How are the Nazi soldiers and officers portrayed by the author? Do any of them share any qualities of any of the other characters?

9. Define climax. Next, summarize the main events leading up to **it** and the remaining events after **it** that create the resolution in this novel.

10. Hannah feels the special magic of Aunt Eva even as a young girl. How is that reinforced after Hannah's return from the time travel?

<u>Critical</u>

11. This novel's title, *The Devil's Arithmetic*, indicates what message to the reader?

12. Of what significance is the story about the 'walking dead' that Hannah tells her brother, Aaron, on the way to their grandparents' apartment?"

13. Compare and contrast life in Europe, especially Poland, during World War II with life there now.

14. Why does Grandma Belle allow Aunt Eva to light the candles for religious and family ceremonies in her own home? How does Hannah come to understand this better?

15. How might the story have changed if Chaya had lived?

16. What does the 'blue ballpoint- pen written- on -the -arm' incident of a younger Hannah reveal about both her and her grandfather?

17. Contrast Hannah's behavior and personality *before* and *after* her time travel to Poland.

18. Why do you think the Nazis posted the sign, 'Work makes you free' on the gates of the camps?

19. For what reason do you think the author introduced the friendship of Rivka and Chaya into the plot?

20. Describe Jane Yolen's writing style, including her use of figurative language. How does it shape the reader's perception of the story? What other type books has this prolific author written? Why would she choose to write a book for young adults on this subject?

21. What implication was there in the retelling of the story of Hansel and Gretel by Chaya to her young girlfriends on the way to the wedding?

22. Compose another title for this novel. What part of the novel lead you to come up with it? (Fact: Devil's Arithmetic was not Yolen's original title)

23. Compare a traditional wedding that you have attended to the pre-wedding festivities held in honor of Fayge and Shmuel's Jewish wedding.

24. Interpret Fayge's tale about the young boy, Israel, and the werewolf's heart at the end of Chapter Sixteen.

25. What did Fayge mean when she threw herself at Shmuel's feet and said, "The sky is our canopy. God's canopy. The sky."?

26. Can you identify any situation in the world today where one group of people is the victim of oppression or discrimination by their government such as the Holocaust?

Critical/ Personal Response
27. Why do you suppose that even though both Gitl and Yitzchak survived the camp and emigrated to Israel, neither of them ever married.

28. Have you read any other books written by Jane Yolen? How do they compare to *The Devil's Arithmetic*? Which one is your favorite? Why?

29. Why do you think the author chose to present this subject matter through a time travel? If you were the author, how would you have presented a story like this?

30. Do you think Hannah and Aaron get along well? Why or why not? Do you get along well with your siblings? Explain.

31. How does Gitl bear witness after her emigration to Israel? Why is this important?

32. When the wedding party comes upon the Nazis, the badchan says, " The snake smiles but it shows no teeth, and "Better the fox to guard the hens and the wolves to guard the sheep." What is the meaning of these proverbs? Can you think of any other ones that would fit the situation?

Personal Response

33. Explain how your perspective would have changed after you went through this experience, if you were Hannah.

34. Rivka reassures Chaya of what a hero is. She says , "My mother said before she died that it is much harder to die this way than to go out shooting. Much harder. Chaya, you are a hero. I am a hero. We are all heroes here." Explain your definition of a hero, giving examples to support it.

35. How do you think you would have handled the horrors and atrocities of the death camps had you been one of its victims?

36. Why does Hannah feel guilty and to blame for Reuven's death? Who do you think is responsible?

37. Yolen's descriptions of the horrors in this book came from authentic sources. Why do you think she was unable to ask these survivors about their experiences? (please see dedication page)

38. Rivka says of the death camp," God is letting it happen, but there is a reason. We cannot see it yet. " Do you think we can see it now?

39. Have you read any other historical fiction from this time period? If so, name them. In what ways are they similar to or different from *The Devil's Arithmetic*?

40. Hannah wants to stay at her Christian friend, Rosemary's, instead of joining her family for their Passover tradition.. Have you ever experienced a parental expectation that is different from your desire? Explain. How did you deal with it?

41. The entire Jewish population was discriminated against in Europe during this time period. Share a time you felt you were discriminated against. Why did you feel you were treated differently and how did you respond?

42. Compare and contrast the Jewish religion's holidays and beliefs to your religion's.

43. Interpret Hannah's memory of the saying, "It's easier to ask for forgiveness than permission."

Quotations
1. "All Jewish holidays are about remembering, Mama. I'm tired of remembering."

2. "I can't remember all four questions. What if I can't read it right?"

3. "I'll give them this!"

4. "Passover isn't about eating. It's about remembering."

5. "Don't be such a baby, Ron-ron. The Four Questions aren't that hard."

6. "Why does he bother with it? It's all in the past. There aren't any concentration camps now. Why bring it up?"

7. "Grandpa Dan wasn't in the camps, thank God. He was born in America, just like you."

8. "A yahrzeit for all the beloved dead, a grace for all the beloved living."

9. "Let Hannahleh join the toasts for real."

10. "Look where I hid the afikoman."

11. "Open the door to Elijah, child, and invite him in with an open heart."

12. "Open it Hannah! Open it for Elijah! "

13. "And do you think the prophet Elijah walks in every time you open a door?"

14. "Being married does not bother me, but getting married -that frightens me. "

15. "We do not follow all the old customs, alone here and so far from the village. But I think it is not bad to hold to some of the traditions, like the groom's wedding fast."

16. "You will wear the dress I wore for as a child for Shmuel's Bar Mitzvah."

17. "We will be married. Your father will marry us. Maybe not here, in your shul. Maybe not even under a wedding canopy."

18. "How can you talk like that? Your words will fly up to heaven and call down the Angel of Death, Lilith's bridegroom, with his poisoned sword."

19. "She is right, child. What is here is bad enough. Let us live moment by moment. There is no harm in dreaming about a shower."

20. "She'd been shorn of memory as brutally as she'd been shorn of her hair, without permission, without reason."

21. "Now my brother Wolf is left, but he is a Sonderkommando, one of the walking dead. He might as well be with them. We all have such stories. It is brutal arithmetic."

22. "I play the man's game. And so I stay alive. Alive I can help you. Dead I am no help to you at all. There are good numbers and bad numbers."

23. "Dr. Mengele. The Angel of Auschwitz."

24. "A boy your age should be with his mother. So I shall be sure you go to her."

25. "God is letting it happen, but there is a reason. We cannot see it yet."

26. "It is much harder to live this way and to die this way than to go out shooting We are all heroes here.."

27. "Then Israel took pity on the heart and gave it freedom. He placed it upon the earth and the earth opened and swallowed the black heart into itself."

28. "The days' routines were as before, the only change being the constant redness of the sky as trainloads of nameless zugangi were shipped along the rails of death. Still the camp seemed curiously lightened because of it, as if everyone knew that as long as others were processed, they would not be. A simple bit of mathematics, like subtraction, where one taken away from the top line becomes one added on to the bottom. The Devil's arithmetic."

29. "Fayge says she prefers the dark wolf she knows to the dark one she does not."

30. "No, they are processed at once, as has been ordered from Berlin. They are part of the Final Solution to the Jewish Problem."

31. "Let them all go up the stack!"

32. "The sky is our canopy. God's canopy. The sky."

33. "How can you remember what has not happened yet? Memory does not work that way- forward. It only works backward.!"

34. "I remember. And you must remember too, so that whoever of us survives this place will carry the message into that future."

35. "Let me tell you a story, a story I know you both will love. It is about a girl. An ordinary sort of girl named....."

36. "J is for Jew. And 1 because you were alone, alone of the 8 who had been in your family......"

37. "In my village, in the camp...in the past, I was called Rivka...."

38. "You are staring at my arm. At the number. Does it frighten you still? You've never let me explain it to you and your mother hates me to talk of it. Still if you want me to..."

LESSON EIGHTEEN

Objectives

    To review all of the vocabulary work done in this unit

Activity

    Choose one (or more) of the vocabulary review activities listed and spend your class period as directed in the activity. Some of the materials for these review activities are located in the Extra Activities Packet in this unit.

VOCABULARY REVIEW ACTIVITIES

1. Divide your class into two teams and have an old-fashioned spelling or definition bee.
2. Give each of your students (or students in groups of two, three or four) a *The Devil's Arithmetic* Vocabulary Word Search Puzzle. The person (group) to find all of the vocabulary words in the puzzle first wins.
3. Give students a *The Devil's Arithmetic* Vocabulary Word Search Puzzle without the word list. The person or group to find the most vocabulary words in the puzzle wins.
4. Use a *The Devil's Arithmetic* Vocabulary Crossword Puzzle. Put the puzzle onto a transparency on the overhead projector (so everyone can see it), and do the puzzle together as a class.
5. Give students a *The Devil's Arithmetic* Vocabulary Matching Worksheet to do.
6. Divide your class into two teams. Use *The Devil's Arithmetic* vocabulary words with their letters jumbled as a word list. Student 1 from Team A faces off against Student 1 from Team B. You write the first jumbled word on the board. The first student (1A or 1B) to unscramble the word wins the chance for his/her team to score points. If 1A wins the jumble, go to student 2A and give him/her a definition. He/she must give you the correct spelling of the vocabulary word which fits that definition. If he/she does, Team A scores a point, and you give student 3A a definition for which you expect a correctly spelled matching vocabulary word. Continue giving Team A definitions until some team member makes an incorrect response. An incorrect response sends the game back to the jumbled -word face off, this time with students 2A and 2B. Instead of repeating giving definitions to the first few students of each team, continue with the student after the one who gave the last incorrect response on the team. For example, if Team B wins the jumbled-word face-off, and student 5B gave the last incorrect answer for Team B, you would start this round of definition questions with student 6B, and so on. The team with the most points wins!
7. Have students write a story in which they correctly use as many vocabulary words as possible. Have students read their compositions orally. Post the most original compositions on your bulletin board.

LESSON NINETEEN

Objective
    To review the main ideas presented in *The Devil's Arithmetic*

Activity #1
    Choose one of the review games/activities included in the packet and spend your class period as outlined there. Some materials for these activities are located in the Extra Activities Packet section of this unit.

Activity #2
    Remind students that the Unit Test will be in the next class meeting. Stress the review of the Study Guides and their class notes as a last minute, brush-up review for the unit test.

REVIEW GAMES/ACTIVITIES - *The Devil's Arithmetic*

1. Ask the class to make up a unit test for *The Devil's Arithmetic*. The test should have 4 sections: matching, true/false, short answer, and essay. Students may use 1/2 period to make the test and then swap papers and use the other 1/2 class period to take a test a classmate has devised (open book). You may want to use the unit test included in this packet or take questions from the students' unit tests to formulate your own test.

2. Take 1/2 period for students to make up true and false questions (including the answers). Collect the papers and divide the class into two teams. Draw a big tic-tac-toe board on the chalk board. Make one team X and one team O. Ask questions to each side, giving each student one turn. If the question is answered correctly, that students' team's letter (X or O) is placed in the box. If the answer is incorrect, no mark is placed in the box. The object is to get three marks in a row like tic-tac-toe. You may want to keep track of the number of games won for each team.

3. Take 1/2 period for students to make up questions (true/false and short answer). Collect the questions. Divide the class into two teams. You'll alternate asking questions to individual members of teams A & B (like in a spelling bee). The question keeps going from A to B until it is correctly answered, then a new question is asked. A correct answer does not allow the team to get another question. Correct answers are +2 points; incorrect answers are -1 point.

4. Have students pair up and quiz each other from their study guides and class notes.

5. Give students a *The Devil's Arithmetic* crossword puzzle to complete.

6. Divide your class into two teams. Use *The Devil's Arithmetic* crossword words with their letters jumbled as a word list. Student 1 from Team A faces off against Student 1 from Team B. You write the first jumbled word on the board. The first student (1A or 1B) to unscramble the word wins the chance for his/her team to score points. If 1A wins the jumble, go to student 2A and give him/her a clue. He/she must give you the correct word which matches that clue. If he/she does, Team A scores a point, and you give student 3A a clue for which you expect another correct response. Continue giving Team A clues until some team member makes an incorrect response. An incorrect response sends the game back to the jumbled-word face off, this time with students 2A and 2B. Instead of repeating giving clues to the first few students of each team, continue with the student after the one who gave the last incorrect response on the team. For example, if Team B wins the jumbled-word face-off, and student 5B gave the last incorrect answer for Team B, you would start this round of clue questions with student 6B, and so on.

UNIT TESTS

LESSON TWENTY

<u>Objective</u>

To test the students understanding of the main ideas and themes in *The Devil's Arithmetic*

<u>Activity #1</u>

Distribute the unit tests. Go over the instructions in detail and allow the students the entire class period to complete the exam.

<u>Activity #2</u>

Collect all test papers and assigned books prior to the end of the class period.

NOTES ABOUT THE UNIT TESTS IN THIS UNIT:

There are 5 different unit tests which follow.

There are two short answer tests which are based primarily on facts from the novel. The answer key for short answer unit test 1 follows the student test. The answer key for short answer test 2 follows the student short answer unit test 2.

There is one advanced short answer unit test. It is based on the extra discussion questions and quotations. Use the matching key for short answer unit test 2 to check the matching section of the advanced short answer unit test. There is no key for the short answer questions and quotations. The answers will be based on the discussions you have had during class.

There are two multiple choice unit tests. Following the two unit tests, you will find an answer sheet on which students should mark their answers. The same answer sheet should be used for both tests; however, students' answers will be different for each test. Following the students' answer sheet for the multiple choice tests you will find your answer keys.

The short answer tests have a vocabulary section. You should choose 10 of the vocabulary words from this unit, read them orally and have the students write them down. Then, either have students write a definition or use the words in sentences.

Use these words for the vocabulary section of the advanced short answer test:

incineration	conspiratorial	periphery
sonorous	undistinguishable	dissipating
amalgam	discernible	desecrate
pervasive	crematoria	mortified

Name_____

SHORT ANSWER UNIT TEST #1 - *The Devil's Arithmetic*

I. Matching/Identify

_____ 1. KOMMANDOS

_____ 2. CHANUKAH

_____ 3. MUSSELMEN

_____ 4. TATTOO

_____ 5. YARMULKES

_____ 6. ELIJAH

_____ 7. J18202

_____ 8. BREUER

_____ 9. SWALLOWS

_____ 10. SCHNELL

_____ 11. HOLOCAUST

_____ 12. RESETTLEMENT

_____ 13. AARON

_____ 14. YITZCHAK

_____ 15. WINE

_____ 16. VIOSK

_____ 17. AUNT EVA

_____ 18. MALACH HA-MAVIS

_____ 19. HAGGADAH

_____ 20. YOLEN

A. Little hats worn by men during ceremony

B. Butcher who escaped camp

C. Angel of Death

D. Chaya's friend Rivka

E. Mass destruction of European Jews

F. Those who give up the fight

G. Sang around the smokestack

H. Removing Jews to the concentration camps

I. Author

J. Called Ron-ron by his big sister Hannah

K. Fayge's Polish village

L. Blue numbers burnt into flesh

M. Made Hannah's head hurt after she drank it

N. Nazi camp commandant

O. Eight day Jewish festival held in December

P. Rivka's number

Q. Apartment door opened to welcome him

R. Jewish guide book

S. Jews made to carry the corpses

T. Yelled constantly to the Jews at the camp

90

II. Short Answer
1. For whom is Hannah named?

2. When Hannah was younger what did she do that she thought would please her Grandpa Will?

3. What does Shmuel admit to Hannah the next morning, the day of his wedding?

4. Why were the shtetl girls especially fascinated with Hannah?

5. What does Hannah tell the rabbi to try to get him to turn back? How does he respond?

6. After getting out of the trucks, what does the Nazi officer demand the villagers to do first?

7. Describe the conditions of the boxcars and the length of time spent in them.

8. What message adorned the iron gates of the camp?

9. Why does Hannah decide not to say anymore about what she remembers about the Holocaust, especially the showers?

10. After her hair is shorn from her head, what does Hannah realize?

11. What command does Hannah impose upon herself to numb the shock?

12. What does Rivka share with the girls about the rest of her family?

13. What job does Hannah have in the camp?

14. Explain Rivka's definition of The Devil's Arithmetic.

15. In what way did Hannah find irony in the everyday events of nature surrounding the camp?

The Devil's Arithmetic Short Answer Unit Test 1 page 4

III. Essay

Explain why you think the author introduced the friendship of Rivka and Chaya into the plot?

IV. Vocabulary
   Listen to the vocabulary word and spell it. After you have spelled all the words, go back and write down the definitions.

1.

2.

3.

4.

5.

6.

7.

8.

9.

10.

93

KEY: SHORT ANSWER UNIT TEST #1 - *The Devil's Arithmetic*

I. Matching/Identify

S - 1. KOMMANDOS   A. Little hats worn by men during ceremony

O - 2. CHANUKAH   B. Butcher who escaped camp

F - 3. MUSSELMEN   C. Angel of Death

L - 4. TATTOO   D. Chaya's friend Rivka

A - 5. YARMULKES   E. Mass destruction of European Jews

Q - 6. ELIJAH   F. Those who give up the fight

P - 7. J18202   G. Sang around the smokestack

N - 8. BREUER   H. Removing Jews to the concentration camps

G - 9. SWALLOWS   I. Author

T - 10. SCHNELL   J. Called Ron-ron by his big sister Hannah

E - 11. HOLOCAUST   K. Fayge's Polish village

H - 12. RESETTLEMENT   L. Blue numbers burnt into flesh

J - 13. AARON   M. Made Hannah's head hurt after she drank it

B - 14. YITZCHAK   N. Nazi camp commandant

M - 15. WINE   O. Eight day Jewish festival held in December

K - 16. VIOSK   P. Rivka's number

D - 17. AUNT EVA   Q. Apartment door opened to welcome him

C - 18. MALACH HA-MAVIS   R. Jewish guide book

R - 19. HAGGADAH   S. Jews made to carry the corpses

I - 20. YOLEN   T. Yelled constantly to the Jews at the camp

94

II. Short Answer
1. For whom is Hannah named?
    She is named for a dead friend of her favorite Aunt Eva's.
2. When Hannah was younger what did she do that she thought would please her Grandpa Will?
    She took a ballpoint pen and wrote numbers on her arm to resemble his concentration camp tattoo.

3. What does Shmuel admit to Hannah the next morning, the day of his wedding?
    He is afraid of *getting* married, but not *being* married to Fayge.

4. Why were the shtetl girls especially fascinated with Hannah?
    They loved her many stories of books she has read and movies she has seen.

5. What does Hannah tell the rabbi to try to get him to turn back? How does he respond?
    She tells him that six million Jews will be killed by the Nazis and he says that it is only God before whom we must tremble.

6. After getting out of the trucks, what does the Nazi officer demand the villagers to do first?
    He orders them to lie down and when they do not move immediately, he fires his gun at their feet to get them to quickly follow his order.

7. Describe the conditions of the boxcars and the length of time spent in them.
    They were kept inside of them for four days and nights with one brief stop for each boxcar. It was like standing in an oven that smelled of human sweat, urine, and feces. Four dead bodies were slung out onto a siding and a dead baby was cast behind a horse watering trough.

8. What message adorned the iron gates of the camp?
    Work makes you free was written on the gates.

9. Why does Hannah decide not to say anymore about what she remembers about the Holocaust, especially the showers?
    She wants to be brave while waiting and not take away the others' hope, which is all they have.

10. After her hair is shorn from her head, what does Hannah realize?
    She has lost her memory. She'd been shorn of her memory as brutally as she'd been shorn of her hair, without permission, without reason. She is startled because all the girls and women look alike with no hair.

11. What command does Hannah impose upon herself to numb the shock?
    Don't think. Do.

12. What does Rivka share with the girls about the rest of her family?
    During the year she has been in the camp, her mother, three sisters, father, and brother have all been sent to the ovens. Her remaining brother, Wolfe, must work as a Sonderkommando, one of the walking dead who handle the corpses..

13. What job does Hannah have in the camp?
    She and Shifre worked in the kitchen with Rivka: hauling water in large buckets, spooning out the meager meals, scrubbing the giant cauldrons, and scrubbing the walls and floors.

14. Explain Rivka's definition of The Devil's Arithmetic.
    She shares that the cruel numbers of those processed and the rest of their remaining days add up or subtract to become the devil's arithmetic.

15. In what way did Hannah find irony in the everyday events of nature surrounding the camp?
    It was as if all nature ignored what went on in the camp. There were bright flowers, brilliant sunsets, and soft breezes. She thought that if this tragedy had been happening in a book, the skies would be weeping and the swallows mourning by the smokestack.

III. Essay
Explain why you think the author introduced the friendship of Rivka and Chaya into the plot.

IV. Vocabulary
Choose ten of the vocabulary words to read orally for the vocabulary section of this unit test.

SHORT ANSWER UNIT TEST 2 *The Devil's Arithmetic*

I. Matching/Identify

_____ 1. CHANUKAH   A. To remember and tell so it won't happen again

_____ 2. MALACH HA-MAVIS   B. Those taken to the fire

_____ 3. BRONX   C. Showers

_____ 4. WINE   D. Matzoh wrapped in blue cloth and hidden

_____ 5. BABUSHKA   E. Eight day Jewish festival held in December

_____ 6. AFIKOMAN   F. Permitted according to Jewish law

_____ 7. RESETTLEMENT   G. Number of days spent in the cattle cars

_____ 8. PASSOVER   H. Cremated

_____ 9. ICE COLD   I. Grandpa Will and Grandma Belle's residence

_____ 10. MIDDEN   J. Annual Jewish feast

_____ 11. CHOSEN   K. Author

_____ 12. J18202   L. Huge soup kettles

_____ 13. CAULDRONS   M. Rivka's number

_____ 14. BEAR WITNESS   N. Angel of Death

_____ 15. FOUR   O. Made Hannah's head hurt after she drank it

_____ 16. PROCESSED   P. Garbage pile where children hid

_____ 17. KOSHER   Q. Newcomers

_____ 18. ZUGANGI   R. Fayge's rabbi father

_____ 19. REB BORUCH   S. Removing Jews to the concentration camps

_____ 20. YOLEN   T. Rivka's kerchief

II. Short Answer
1. Why does the Stern family open the door to admit the prophet Elijah?

2. How do Gitl and Shmuel react to Hannah's ravings about her coming from New Rochelle, New York?

3. After getting out of the trucks, what does the Nazi officer demand the villagers to do first?

4. Why does Hannah decide not to say anymore about what she remembers about the Holocaust, especially the showers?

5. What command does Hannah impose upon herself to numb the shock?

6. When Gitl tries to leave the barracks to find something to eat for the children, what does the young soldier tell her?

7. What message does the officer give to the newcomers after they have eaten?

8. What does Rivka share with the girls about the rest of her family?

9. What is the signal for the young children that the commandant is coming?

10. How does Rivka respond when Hannah suggests that they should at least go down fighting.

11. How did Fayge react to Shmuel's impending punishment?

12. What was Hannah trying to tell the girls when the new guard confronted them?

13. Which three girls does the young officer choose? How does Hannah change the course of events?

14. When Aunt Eva wants to explain the meaning of the tattoo, how does Hannah surprise her?

15. What does Aunt Eva share with Hannah about her past when they were alone?

III. Essay
Why do you think the Nazis posted the sign, 'Work makes you free' on the gates of the camps?

Vocabulary
   Listen to the vocabulary word and spell it. After you have spelled all the words, go back and write down the definitions.

    1.

    2.

    3.

    4.

    5.

    6.

    7.

    8.

    9.

    10.

KEY: SHORT ANSWER UNIT TEST 2 *The Devil's Arithmetic*

I. Matching

E - 1. CHANUKAH

N - 2. MALACH HA-MAVIS

I - 3. BRONX

O - 4. WINE

T - 5. BABUSHKA

D - 6. AFIKOMAN

S - 7. RESETTLEMENT

J - 8. PASSOVER

C - 9. ICE COLD

P - 10. MIDDEN

B - 11. CHOSEN

M - 12. J18202

L - 13. CAULDRONS

A - 14. BEAR WITNESS

G - 15. FOUR

H - 16. PROCESSED

F - 17. KOSHER

Q - 18. ZUGANGI

R - 19. REB BORUCH

K - 20. YOLEN

A. To remember and tell so it won't happen again

B. Those taken to the fire

C. Showers

D. Matzoh wrapped in blue cloth and hidden

E. Eight day Jewish festival held in December

F. Permitted according to Jewish law

G. Number of days spent in the cattle cars

H. Cremated

I. Grandpa Will and Grandma Belle's residence

J. Annual Jewish feast

K. Author

L. Huge soup kettles

M. Rivka's number

N. Angel of Death

O. Made Hannah's head hurt after she drank it

P. Garbage pile where children hid

Q. Newcomers

R. Fayge's rabbi father

S. Removing Jews to the concentration camps

T. Rivka's kerchief

II. Short Answer
1. Why does the family open the door to admit the prophet Elijah?
    It is a tradition to remind themselves of the time Jews were forced to keep their doors open to show the Christians they were not practicing blood rituals.

2. How do Gitl and Shmuel react to Hannah's ravings about her coming from New Rochelle, New York?
    They think her illness has affected her mentally. They are certain she is their niece, Chaya, from Lublin.

3. After getting out of the trucks, what does the Nazi officer demand the villagers to do first?
    He orders them to lie down and when they do not move immediately, he fires his gun at their feet to get them to quickly follow his order.

4. Why does Hannah decide not to say anymore about what she remembers about the Holocaust, especially the showers?
    She wants to be brave while waiting and not take away the others' hope, which is all they have.

5. What command does Hannah impose upon herself to numb the shock?
    Don't think. Do.

6. When Gitl tries to leave the barracks to find something to eat for the children, what does the young soldier tell her?
    He says, "they will get used to it." He then points to the smokestack saying, "That is Jew smoke. Learn to eat when it's given to you, Jew, or you, too, go up that stack."

7. What message does the officer give to the newcomers after they have eaten?
    You will work hard, never answer back, complain, or question or try to escape. All this will be done for the Fatherland.

8. What does Rivka share with the girls about the rest of her family?
    During the year she has been in the camp, her mother, three sisters, father, and brother have all been sent to the ovens. Her remaining brother, Wolfe, must work as a Sonderkommando, one of the walking dead who handle the corpses.

9. What is the signal for the young children that the commandant is coming?
    The older children and adults make a clucking noise by placing their tongues against the roof of their mouths.

10. How does Rivka respond when Hannah suggests that they should at least go down fighting.
    She responds with , "It is harder to die this way than to go out shooting. We are all heroes here."
11. How did Fayge react to Shmuel's impending punishment?
    She pushed through the crowd and flung herself at this feet.

12. What was Hannah trying to tell the girls when the new guard confronted them?
    She was remembering history and parts of her former life. She was pleading with the girls to be certain to carry the message into the future to prevent what was happening there from ever happening again. They were perplexed with her talk and questioned her.

13. Which three girls does the young officer choose? How does Hannah change the course of events?
    He picks Esther, Shifre, and Rivka. Rivka asks Hannah, "Who will remember for you now?" She removes the kerchief from Rivka's head, ties it hastily on hers, and takes her place with Esther and Shifre. She softly commands Rivka to "Run for her life, Run for her future, And to Remember.

14. When Aunt Eva wants to explain the meaning of the tattoo, how does Hannah surprise her?
    Hannah recognizes the number as Rivka's number and wants to explain what she has learned to her aunt. It is then that she realizes that (Aunt Eva) Rivka's brother, Wolfe, is her Grandpa Will.

15. What does Aunt Eva share with Hannah about her past when they were alone?
    She tells Hannah that of all the villagers Chaya had come to the camp with, only Gitl and Yitzchak survived. They both emigrated to Israel and remained close friends, until well into their seventies. Neither married and both thrived to bear witness

III. Essay
Why do you think the Nazis posted the sign, 'Work makes you free' on the gates of the camps?

IV. Vocabulary
Choose ten of the vocabulary words to read orally for the vocabulary section of the test.

ADVANCED SHORT ANSWER UNIT TEST - *The Devil's Arithmetic*

I. Matching

_____ 1. CHANUKAH

_____ 2. MALACH HA-MAVIS

_____ 3. BRONX

_____ 4. WINE

_____ 5. BABUSHKA

_____ 6. AFIKOMAN

_____ 7. RESETTLEMENT

_____ 8. PASSOVER

_____ 9. ICE COLD

_____ 10. MIDDEN

_____ 11. CHOSEN

_____ 12. J18202

_____ 13. CAULDRONS

_____ 14. BEAR WITNESS

_____ 15. FOUR

_____ 16. PROCESSED

_____ 17. KOSHER

_____ 18. ZUGANGI

_____ 19. REB BORUCH

_____ 20. YOLEN

A. To remember and tell so it won't happen again

B. Those taken to the fire

C. Showers

D. Matzoh wrapped in blue cloth and hidden

E. Eight day Jewish festival held in December

F. Permitted according to Jewish law

G. Number of days spent in the cattle cars

H. Cremated

I. Grandpa Will and Grandma Belle's residence

J. Annual Jewish feast

K. Author

L. Huge soup kettles

M. Rivka's number

N. Angel of Death

O. Made Hannah's head hurt after she drank it

P. Garbage pile where children hid

Q. Newcomers

R. Fayge's rabbi father

S. Removing Jews to the concentration camps

T. Rivka's kerchief

II. Short Answer

1. Of what significance is the story about the 'walking dead' that Hannah tells her brother, Aaron, on the way to their grandparents' apartment?"

2. How might the story have changed if Chaya had lived?

3. Why do you think the Nazis posted the sign, 'Work makes you free' on the gates of the camps?

4. For what reason do you think the author introduced the friendship of Rivka and Chaya into the plot?

5. What did Fayge mean when she threw herself at Shmuel's feet and said, "The sky is our canopy. God's canopy. The sky."?

6. When the wedding party comes upon the Nazis, the badchan says, " The snake smiles but it shows no teeth, and "Better the fox to guard the hens and the wolves to guard the sheep." In simple terms, what is the meaning of these proverbs?

III. Essay
Interpret the following excerpt from the novel. "A simple bit of mathematics, like subtraction, where one taken away from the top line becomes one added on to the bottom. The Devil's Arithmetic."

IV. Vocabulary
Listen to the vocabulary words and write them down. After you have written down all the words, write a paragraph in which you use all the words. The paragraph must in some way relate to *The Devil's Arithmetic*.

MULTIPLE CHOICE-MATCHING UNIT TEST 1 - *The Devil's Arithmetic*

I. Matching

_____ 1. CLUCKING

A. 5701 according to the Jewish calendar

_____ 2. 1942

B. Number of days spent in the cattle cars

_____ 3. FAYGE

C. Rivka's number

_____ 4. SEDER

D. Called Ron-ron by his big sister Hannah

_____ 5. WINE

E. Spoken and understood by Chaya Abramowicz

_____ 6. AARON

F. Grandpa Will and Grandma Belle's residence

_____ 7. HANNAH

G. Showers

_____ 8. BREUER

H. Shmuel's fiance

_____ 9. FOUR

I. Warning sound to children to hide

_____ 10. BRONX

J. Nazi camp commandant

_____ 11. J18202

K. Blue numbers burnt into flesh

_____ 12. TATTOO

L. Time travels to Polish village in 1940's

_____ 13. CLOTHES BASKET

M. Means order

_____ 14. ICE COLD

N. Where Aaron hid the afikoman

_____ 15. YIDDISH

O. Made Hannah's head hurt after she drank it

II. Multiple Choice

1. Why was Hannah's younger brother scared?
    a. He never rode through New York City before that day.
    b. He was to read the Four Questions from the Haggadah.
    c. He never met all the relatives that were going to be at his house.
    d. He would be the first one to find the afikoman.

2. For whom is Hannah named?
    a. She is named for her favorite aunt.
    b. She is named for her grandmother.
    c. She is named for a dead friend of her favorite Aunt Eva's.
    d. She is named for her father's mother.

3. When Hannah was younger what did she do that she thought would please her Grandpa Will?
    a. She memorized the Four Questions from the Haggadah.
    b. She took a ballpoint pen and wrote numbers on her arm.
    c. She baked him his favorite cake and it flopped.
    d. She crawled up in his lap and recited the Seder.

4. Grandfather Will decides that Hannah is old enough to
    a. partake of the wine toasting.
    b. open the door for Elijah.
    c. recite from memory the Four Questions.
    d. none of the above

5. When Hannah raves about living in New Rochelle Gitl and Shmuel
    a. think her illness has taken its toll on her.
    b. are ready to send her back to Lublin.
    c. want to take her back to Lublin to visit to be able to remember.
    d. regret having taken her in after her parents died.

6. What does Gitl tell Hannah to wear to the wedding?
    a. She tells her to wear the blue sailor-suit dress she wore to Shmuel's Bar Mitzvah.
    b. A dress Hannah says is a rag.
    c. A dress Hannah thinks is suitable for a Halloween party.
    d. All of the above

7. What quick observation does the badchan make of Hannah?
    a. He sees that she is dressed in a dress she doesn't like.
    b. He can tell she is different from the other girls.
    c. He looks into her eyes and sees the future.
    d. He calls her wise and an old girl in young-girl disguise.

8. When the wedding party approaches the village they see
    a. that the two lovebirds are wandering off to be alone.
    b. the rest of the village waiting for the ceremony.
    c. trucks and automobiles parked in front of the shul.
    d. that the synagogue is on fire.

9. Hannah is able to determine what is going to happen next because
    a. she can remember the history she has studied.
    b. the Nazi soldiers remind her of the TV program.
    c. she didn't really live there, she used to live in Lublin.
    d. she saw the Nazis in Lublin where they did the same thing to her village.

10. Hannah tells the rabbi
    a. to turn the wagons back.
    b. that six million Jews will die.
    c. not to ask her how she knows, she just does.
    d. all of the above

11. What message adorns the gates of the camp?
    a. All work is done for the Fatherland.
    b. Work is good for you.
    c. All work and no play every day.
    d. Work will set you free.

12. Hannah speaks out and questions the woman guard so she
    a. is slapped on both cheeks.
    b. must surrender her blue hair ribbons.
    c. is denied her first meal.
    d. both a and b

13. After Hannah's hair has been shorn, she realizes
    a. she has lost her memory along with her hair.
    b. she cannot recall Gitl or Shmuel's name.
    c. she cannot find her friends, Rachel and Esther.
    d. both a and c

14. Select the one thing the man who tattooed Hannah did not tell her.
    a. He bought the dress in Lublin for his daughter, Chaya.
    b. She is wearing his daughter's dress.
    c. She has the same name as his daughter.
    d. She is the same age as his daughter.

15. All of Rivka's family has been sent to the ovens since their arrival a year ago.
    a. true
    b. false

16. Select which rule Rivka says is the most important rule of survival in the camp.
    a. Help the little ones hide in the midden.
    b. Organize.
    c. Learn to read other prisoners' numbers.
    d. Do not ask why.

17. Hannah feels that Reuven's choosing was her fault because
    a. she should have warned him the officer was coming.
    b. she could have thrown herself over him to hide him.
    c. she didn't get him into the midden fast enough.
    d. she thinks she should have told the commandant he was her brother.

18. Rivka's response to Hannah's outrage that they should go down fighting is
    a. one of agreement.
    b. Both c and d
    c. We are all heroes here.
    d. It is harder to die this way than to go down fighting.

19. Fayge was made to watch her beloved's execution.
    a. true
    b. false

20. How many more bodies were needed to make a full load, according to the new guard?
    a. five
    b. two
    c. four
    d. three

110

III. Quotations: Identify the speaker:

A= Aaron   B= Rivka   C= Fayge   D = Nazi
E=Gitl   F= Shmuel   G= Aunt Eva   H= Hannah

1. "You are staring at my arm. At the number. Does it frighten you still? You've never let me explain it to you and your mother hates me to talk of it. Still if you want me to..."

2. "Why does he bother with it? It's all in the past. There aren't any concentration camps now. Why bring it up?"

3. "Look where I hid the afikoman."

4. "Open it Hannah! Open it for Elijah! "

5. "Being married does not bother me, but getting married -that frightens me. "

6. "You will wear the dress I wore for as a child for Shmuel's Bar Mitzvah."

7. "We will be married. Your father will marry us. Maybe not here, in your shul. Maybe not even under a wedding canopy."

8. "Now my brother Wolfe is left, but he is a Sonderkommando, one of the walking dead. He might as well be with them. We all have such stories. It is brutal arithmetic."

9. "I play the man's game. And so I stay alive. Alive I can help you. Dead I am no help to you at all. There are good numbers and bad numbers."

10. "A boy your age should be with his mother. So I shall be sure you go to her."

11. "It is much harder to live this way and to die this way than to go out shooting We are all heroes here.."

12. "Then Israel took pity on the heart and gave it freedom. He placed it upon the earth and the earth opened and swallowed the black heart into itself."

IV. Vocabulary (Matching)

_____ 1. PORTENTS

_____ 2. CREMATORIA

_____ 3. COMPANIONABLE

_____ 4. IRONY

_____ 5. DESECRATE

_____ 6. DISTORTED

_____ 7. AFFIRMATION

_____ 8. LUMINOUS

_____ 9. INCINERATION

_____ 10. CONSPIRATORIAL

_____ 11. PERIPHERY

_____ 12. FERVOR

_____ 13. BURNISHED

_____ 14. ROUTINIZATION

_____ 15. OMINOUS

_____ 16. DEHUMANIZED

_____ 17. ALIENATED

_____ 18. VEHEMENCE

_____ 19. UNDECIPHERABLE

_____ 20. AMALGAM

A. Heated emotion

B. Polished; waxed

C. Friendly; agreeable

D. Indications; omens

E. Threatening

F. Contradiction

G. Deprived of human dignity

H. Secretly plotting

I. Ruin; violate

J. Unable to solve

K. Distances

L. Passion; intensity

M. Burning

N. Approval

O. Deformed; twisted

P. Mixture

Q. Put into a system

R. Furnace used for cremation

S. Edge; fringe

T. Bright; shining

112

MULTIPLE CHOICE-MATCHING UNIT TEST 2 - *The Devil's Arithmetic*

I. Matching

_____ 1. J18202   A. Mass destruction of European Jews

_____ 2. SEDER   B. Butcher who escaped camp

_____ 3. BREUER   C. Fayge's rabbi father

_____ 4. FOUR QUESTIONS   D. Number of villagers to survive camp

_____ 5. MALACH HA-MAVIS   E. Means order

_____ 6. YITZCHAK   F. Read by Aaron out of the Haggadah for the Seder

_____ 7. WINE   G. Called Ron-ron by his big sister Hannah

_____ 8. BRONX   H. Made Hannah's head hurt after she drank it

_____ 9. BEAR WITNESS   I. Rivka's number

_____ 10. REB BORUCH   J. Shmuel's fiance

_____ 11. TWO   K. Time travels to Polish village in 1940's

_____ 12. AARON   L. To remember and tell so it won't happen again

_____ 13. HOLOCAUST   M. Angel of Death

_____ 14. HANNAH   N. Nazi camp commandant

_____ 15. FAYGE   O. Grandpa Will and Grandma Belle's residence

II. Multiple Choice

1. What is Hannah's complaint to her mother?
   a. She wants to celebrate Easter with Rosemary.
   b. She can't find her best sweater to wear to the Seder.
   c. She wants to go with Rosemary to the movies.
   d. She doesn't want to go to the Seder dinner of Passover at her grandparents.

113

2. For whom is Hannah named?
    a. She is named for her favorite aunt.
    b. She is named for her grandmother.
    c. She is named for a dead friend of her favorite Aunt Eva's.
    d. She is named for her father's mother.

3. What has Grandpa Will so upset?
    a. He is watching a television newscast showing footage from the Holocaust.
    b. He is mad because everyone is late, as usual.
    c. He can't remember what his name was when he was in the death camp.

4. The shtetl girls wish they could go
    a. shopping on weekends.
    b. go to school like Hannah does.
    c. cut their hair like married girls.
    d. watch movies.

5. What does the badchan remind Hannah of?
    a. a priest
    b. a fortuneteller
    c. a jester
    d. a clown

6. To calm their fears, the Jews in the trucks
    a. knelt down and prayed.
    b. sang a kidnapping song loudly.
    c. both a and b
    d. none of the above

7. Which of the following did not happen on the way to resettlement?
    a. Each boxcar was given two stops along the way.
    b. Stories were shared of other horrible treatment of Jews at the hands of Nazis.
    c. The boxcars smelled of human sweat, urine, and feces.
    d. Dead people and a baby were slung out of the boxcars like they were of no value.

8. What message adorns the gates of the camp?
    a. All work is done for the Fatherland.
    b. Work is good for you.
    c. All work and no play every day.
    d. Work will set you free.

9. Hannah speaks out and questions the woman guard so she
    a. is slapped on both cheeks.
    b. must surrender her blue hair ribbons.
    c. is denied her first meal.
    d. both a and b

10. After the group of women and girls undress for the shower, why doesn't Hannah share her memories?
    a. She is afraid of the blue-coated woman guard's temper.
    b. She wants to forget all the painful information she has stored.
    c. She wishes to allow the rest their hope, since it is all they have.
    d. No one asked her to.

11. After Hannah's hair has been shorn, she realizes
    a. she has lost her memory along with her hair.
    b. she cannot recall Gitl or Shmuel's name.
    c. she cannot find her friends, Rachel and Esther.
    d. both a and c

12. Select the one thing the man who tattooed Hannah did not tell her.
    a. He bought the dress in Lublin for his daughter, Chaya.
    b. She is wearing his daughter's dress.
    c. She has the same name as his daughter.
    d. She is the same age as his daughter.

13. Rivka tells the newcomers to use their Every Bowl for
    a. all of the below.
    b. washing.
    c. eating.
    d. drinking.

14. Select which rule Rivka says is the most important rule of survival in the camp.
    a. Help the little ones hide in the midden.
    b. Organize.
    c. Learn to read other prisoners' numbers.
    d. Do not ask why.

15. Fayge's story of the werewolf's heart full of pain is
    a. far above all the girls' understanding.
    b. meant to tell of the earth's wickedness and her pain at the loss of her father.
    c. is a strange tale to have been told by a rabbi.
    d. all of the above

16. Who is the Kommando carrying Fayge's body?
    a. He is Rivka's brother, Wolfe.
    b. He is just another one of the same cruel boys.
    c. He is boy form the village where Esther lived.
    d. He is a Nazi who wants to be an officer.

17. Which of the following is not chosen?
    a. Esther
    b. Rivka
    c. Shifre
    d. Chaya

18. Whose place does Chaya secretly take?
    a. Esther's
    b. Rivka's
    c. Shifre's
    d. Rachel's

19. Hannah learns from her Aunt Eva that
    a. Gitl dies in the camp.
    b. Grandpa Will was the Kommando who carried Fayge's body.
    c. Gitl and Yitzchak lived a long life in Israel.
    d. Both b and c

20. Emmanuel Ringelblum, Jewish historian, claims there were the victories of the camps.
    a. true
    b. false

III. Quotations: Identify the speaker:

A= Hannah   B= Aunt Eva   C= Gitl   D= Shmuel
E= Fayge   F= Nazi   G= Rivka   H= Aaron

1. "You are staring at my arm. At the number. Does it frighten you still? You've never let me explain it to you and your mother hates me to talk of it. Still if you want me to..."

2. "Why does he bother with it? It's all in the past. There aren't any concentration camps now. Why bring it up?"

3. "Look where I hid the afikoman."

4. "Open it Hannah! Open it for Elijah! "

5. "Being married does not bother me, but getting married -that frightens me. "

6. "You will wear the dress I wore for as a child for Shmuel's Bar Mitzvah."

7. "We will be married. Your father will marry us. Maybe not here, in your shul. Maybe not even under a wedding canopy."

8. "Now my brother Wolfe is left, but he is a Sonderkommando, one of the walking dead. He might as well be with them. We all have such stories. It is brutal arithmetic."

9. "I play the man's game. And so I stay alive. Alive I can help you. Dead I am no help to you at all. There are good numbers and bad numbers."

10. "A boy your age should be with his mother. So I shall be sure you go to her."

11. "It is much harder to live this way and to die this way than to go out shooting We are all heroes here.."

12. "Then Israel took pity on the heart and gave it freedom. He placed it upon the earth and the earth opened and swallowed the black heart into itself."

IV. Vocabulary (Matching)

_____ 1. DISCERNIBLE   A. Deep; full sounded

_____ 2. VIGOR   B. Bright; shining

_____ 3. DESECRATE   C. Attention drawn to

_____ 4. RELENTLESSLY   D. Disappearing

_____ 5. ROUTINIZATION   E. Put into a system

_____ 6. VULNERABLE   F. Contradiction

_____ 7. DISSIPATING   G. Skimpy

_____ 8. UNDECIPHERABLE   H. Friendly; agreeable

_____ 9. COMPANIONABLE   I. Defenseless; exposed

_____ 10. SONOROUS   J. Recognizable

_____ 11. MEAGER   K. Passion; intensity

_____ 12. CONSPIRATORIAL   L. Made without yeast

_____ 13. COMPENSATION   M. Deformed; twisted

_____ 14. IRONY   N. Ruin; violate

_____ 15. UNLEAVENED   O. Unable to solve

_____ 16. DISTORTED   P. Reduction

_____ 17. VEHEMENCE   Q. Benefits

_____ 18. LUMINOUS   R. Secretly plotting

_____ 19. RIVETED   S. Energy

_____ 20. COMPRESSION   T. Steadily; constantly

ANSWER SHEET - *The Devil's Arithmetic*
Multiple Choice Unit Tests

I. Matching
1. ____
2. ____
3. ____
4. ____
5. ____
6. ____
7. ____
8. ____
9. ____
10. ____
11. ____
12. ____
13. ____
14. ____
15. ____

II. Multiple Choice
1. (A) (B) (C) (D)
2. (A) (B) (C) (D)
3. (A) (B) (C) (D)
4. (A) (B) (C) (D)
5. (A) (B) (C) (D)
6. (A) (B) (C) (D)
7. (A) (B) (C) (D)
8. (A) (B) (C) (D)
9. (A) (B) (C) (D)
10. (A) (B) (C) (D)
11. (A) (B) (C) (D)
12. (A) (B) (C) (D)
13. (A) (B) (C) (D)
14. (A) (B) (C) (D)
15. (A) (B) (C) (D)
16. (A) (B) (C) (D)
17. (A) (B) (C) (D)
18. (A) (B) (C) (D)
19. (A) (B) (C) (D)
20. (A) (B) (C) (D)

III. Quotes
1. (A) (B) (C) (D) (E) (F) (G) (H)
2. (A) (B) (C) (D) (E) (F) (G) (H)
3. (A) (B) (C) (D) (E) (F) (G) (H)
4. (A) (B) (C) (D) (E) (F) (G) (H)
5. (A) (B) (C) (D) (E) (F) (G) (H)
6. (A) (B) (C) (D) (E) (F) (G) (H)
7. (A) (B) (C) (D) (E) (F) (G) (H)
8. (A) (B) (C) (D) (E) (F) (G) (H)
9. (A) (B) (C) (D) (E) (F) (G) (H)
10. (A) (B) (C) (D) (E) (F) (G) (H)
11. (A) (B) (C) (D) (E) (F) (G) (H)
12. (A) (B) (C) (D) (E) (F) (G) (H)

IV. Vocabulary
1. ____
2. ____
3. ____
4. ____
5. ____
6. ____
7. ____
8. ____
9. ____
10. ____
11. ____
12. ____
13. ____
14. ____
15. ____
16. ____
17. ____
18. ____
19. ____
20. ____

ANSWER SHEET KEY - *Devil's Arithmetic*
Multiple Choice Unit Test 1

I. Matching

1.   I
2.   A
3.   H
4.   M
5.   O
6.   D
7.   L
8.   J
9.   B
10.   F
11.   C
12.   K
13.   N
14.   G
15.   E

II. Multiple Choice

1. (A) ( ) (C) (D)
2. (A) (B) ( ) (D)
3. (A) ( ) (C) (D)
4. ( ) (B) (C) (D)
5. ( ) (B) (C) (D)
6. (A) (B) (C) ( )
7. (A) (B) (C) ( )
8. (A) (B) ( ) (D)
9. ( ) (B) (C) (D)
10. (A) (B) (C) ( )
11. (A) (B) (C) ( )
12. (A) (B) (C) ( )
13. ( ) (B) (C) (D)
14. (A) (B) (C) ( )
15. (A) ( ) (C) (D)
16. (A) (B) ( ) (D)
17. (A) (B) (C) ( )
18. (A) ( ) (C) (D)
19. (A) ( ) (C) (D)
20. (A) (B) (C) ( )

III. Quotes

1. (A) (B) (C) (D) (E) (F) ( ) (H)
2. (A) (B) (C) (D) (E) (F) (G) ( )
3. ( ) (B) (C) (D) (E) (F) (G) (H)
4. ( ) (B) (C) (D) (E) (F) (G) (H)
5. (A) (B) (C) (D) (E) ( ) (G) (H)
6. (A) (B) (C) (D) ( ) (F) (G) (H)
7. (A) (B) (C) (D) (E) ( ) (G) (H)
8. (A) ( ) (C) (D) (E) (F) (G) (H)
9. (A) ( ) (C) (D) (E) (F) (G) (H)
10. (A) (B) (C) ( ) (E) (F) (G) (H)
11. (A) ( ) (C) (D) (E) (F) (G) (H)
12. (A) (B) ( ) (D) (E) (F) (G) (H)

V. Vocabulary

1.   D
2.   R
3.   C
4.   F
5.   I
6.   O
7.   N
8.   T
9.   M
10.   H
11.   S
12.   A
13.   B
14.   Q
15.   E
16.   G
17.   K
18.   L
19.   J
20.   P

ANSWER SHEET KEY - *Devil's Arithmetic*
Multiple Choice Unit Test 2

I. Matching
1.   I
2.   E
3.   N
4.   F
5.   M
6.   B
7.   H
8.   O
9.   L
10. C
11. D
12. G
13. A
14. K
15. J

II. Multiple Choice
1. (A) (B) (C) ( )
2. (A) (B) ( ) (D)
3. ( ) (B) (C) (D)
4. (A) ( ) (C) (D)
5. (A) (B) ( ) (D)
6. (A) ( ) (C) (D)
7. ( ) (B) (C) (D)
8. (A) (B) (C) ( )
9. (A) (B) (C) ( )
10. (A) (B) ( ) (D)
11. ( ) (B) (C) (D)
12. (A) (B) (C) ( )
13. ( ) (B) (C) (D)
14. (A) (B) ( ) (D)
15. (A) ( ) (C) (D)
16. ( ) (B) (C) (D)
17. (A) (B) (C) ( )
18. (A) ( ) (C) (D)
19. (A) ( ) (C) (D)
20. ( ) (B) (C) (D)

III. Quotes
1. (A) ( ) (C) (D) (E) (F) (G) (H)
2. ( ) (B) (C) (D) (E) (F) (G) (H)
3. (A) (B) (C) (D) (E) (F) (G) ( )
4. (A) (B) (C) (D) (E) (F) (G) ( )
5. (A) (B) (C) ( ) (E) (F) (G) (H)
6. (A) (B) ( ) (D) (E) (F) (G) (H)
7. (A) (B) (C) ( ) (E) (F) (G) (H)
8. (A) (B) (C) (D) (E) (F) ( ) (H)
9. (A) (B) (C) (D) (E) (F) ( ) (H)
10. (A) (B) (C) (D) (E) ( ) (G) (H)
11. (A) (B) (C) (D) (E) (F) ( ) (H)
12. (A) (B) (C) (D) ( ) (F) (G) (H)

V. Vocabulary
1.   J
2.   S
3.   N
4.   T
5.   E
6.   I
7.   D
8.   O
9.   H
10. A
11. G
12. R
13. Q
14. F
15. L
16. M
17. K
18. B
19. C
20. P

121

UNIT RESOURCE MATERIALS

BULLETIN BOARD IDEAS - *The Devil's Arithmetic*

1. Save a space for students' best writing. Make a nice border (maybe something from the novel like large numbers and letters jumbled in a variety of ways.) Label the area with the title *The Devil's Arithmetic*. Staple up the best writing samples (or quizzes or whatever you have graded) on colorful paper.

2. Bring in (or have students bring in) pictures of Jewish symbols, Polish villages, traditional family meal table settings, trains on railroad tracks, etc. Make a collage if you have enough different pictures (or post individual pictures on colorful paper if you only have a few pictures). This could also be an introductory activity for students to create a quick bulletin board.

3. Draw one of the word search puzzles onto the bulletin board. (Be sure to enlarge it.) Write the key words to one side. Invite students to take their pens or markers and find the words before and/or after class (or perhaps this could be an activity for students who finish their work early).

4. Have artistic students create a mural depicting the different areas of the concentration camp, etc. Less artistic, but interested students, could do the research from the book to give to the artists for authenticity.

5. Students could create poems using the outline of the Star of David for the basis. They could include words and phrases associated with their concept of this symbol. These could be posted for display.

6. Duplicate the Yiddish words used in the novel. Make a large display listing their English counterparts and an illustration for each.

7. Compare life in Poland during World War II with your students' lives. Have them come up with a list of major differences, advantages, disadvantages, etc. Have them illustrate the differences and display in a creative manner.

8. Artistic students could illustrate some of the scenes from the novel. For example, the crowded conditions in the cattle cars, the shearing of the heads, or the midden where the children hid.

9. Review on a U.S. and world map the location of the Bronx and New Rochelle, New York and the Eastern European country of Poland

10. Portray the main characters and display surrounded with appropriate items that demonstrate their individuality.

11. Hannah's father's family has no photographs of themselves until after the Holocaust. Create family photograph albums, including as many older photographs as possible to share with the class.

EXTRA ACTIVITIES

One of the difficulties in teaching a novel is that all students don't read at the same speed. One student who likes to read may take the book home and finish it in a day or two. Sometimes a few students finish the in-class assignments early. The problem, then, is finding suitable extra activities for students.

One thing that helps is to keep a little library in the classroom. For this unit on *The Devil's Arithmetic*, you might check out from the school library other books by Jane Yolen. A biography of the author would be interesting for some students. You may include other related books and articles about: World War II, the Jewish religion and practices, concentration camps, Yiddish language, Hitler, Nazis, death camps, Holocaust, Holocaust survivors, Holocaust museum, etc.

Other things you may keep on hand are puzzles. We have made some relating directly to *The Devil's Arithmetic* for you. Feel free to duplicate them.

Some students may like to draw. You might devise a contest or allow some extra-credit grade for students who draw characters or scenes from *The Devil's Arithmetic*. Note, too, that if the students do not want to keep their drawings you may pick up some extra bulletin board materials this way. If you have a contest and you supply the prize or, you could possibly make the drawing itself a non-refundable entry fee.

The pages which follow contain games, puzzles and worksheets. The keys, when appropriate, immediately follow the puzzle or worksheet. There are two main groups of activities: one group for the unit; that is, generally relating to *The Devil's Arithmetic* text, and another group of activities related strictly to *The Devil's Arithmetic* vocabulary.

Directions for the games, puzzles and worksheets are self-explanatory. The object here is to provide you with extra materials you may use in any way you choose.

MORE ACTIVITIES - *The Devil's Arithmetic*

1. Pick a chapter or scene with a great deal of dialogue and have the students act it out on a stage. (Perhaps you could assign various scenes to different groups of students so more than one scene could be acted and more students could participate.)

2. Create acrostic poems for the title *The Devil's Arithmetic*.

3. Have students design a book cover (front and back and inside flaps) for *The Devil's Arithmetic*.

4. Research more thoroughly the horrible conditions in the concentration camps. Write letters to unidentified German Nazi commandants protesting the treatment of Jews.

5. Research the Christian Easter traditions and compare them to the Jewish Passover traditions.

6. Use some of the related topics (noted earlier for an in-class library) as topics for research, reports or written papers, or as topics for guest speakers.

7. Have students plan and teach a lesson on a chapter or section of the book. Give them guidelines and a time-frame.

8. Hold a *capsulized version* day. Just like Hannah capsulized her favorite movies, books, and stories for the Polish shtetl girls, have students do the same for their favorites and then share with the class.

9. Discuss the value of family and religious traditions.

10. Write to Jane Yolen asking her questions students have composed. You could send a class set of letters in one large envelope.

11. Invite a Holocaust survivor in to address the class. If no one is available, read aloud to the class the book, *Night* by Elie Wiesel , Holocaust survivor .

12. Show some films that have similar settings or themes such as: Disney Channel's *Friendship in Vienna*, or Columbia Tri-Star's *Alan and Naomi*, or *Escape from Sobibor*. All of these movies display courageous young people during this time period. Students could watch them and then compare them to *The Devil's Arithmetic*.

13. Allow students to select a character from the novel. Have them dress like them, speak like them; assume their persona. Create a talk show format with these characters as the guests. Have a student volunteer to be the host. Others not involved will be the audience, questioning the characters. Select a topic like: cruelty, courage, loyalty, risking your life for another, etc. - themes encountered in the novel. Allow the class to decide as much as possible. Have questions from the audience ready prior to the show day. You could have students try out for

the parts. Remind them to keep it on the up and up, not to mimic some of the seedier talk shows. This will require students to take an in-depth look into the characterization in the novel.

14. Discuss ways to respectfully handle the boredom or irritation young people experience when faced with traditional ceremonies or get-togethers like Hannah hated to attend.

15. If feasible, take the class to a memorial or museum honoring victims of the Holocaust such as the National Holocaust Museum in Washington D. C.

16. Encourage students to read some other timely pieces such as: *Number the Stars, Diary of a Young Girl, The Upstairs Room, Friedrich, Briar Rose, Stepping on the Cracks, Rose Blanche,* etc.

17. Students who like board games may want to create one using information from this novel. Some students could work together as a group to complete this task. Encourage them to look at setting to illustrate their board and possibly use vocabulary, characters, plot, etc. for question cards.

18. Look up the Yiddish words used in the text and find their English counterparts.

19. Watered down salty- tasting potato soup was the daily fare in the camp. Look up and share a variety of soup recipes and perhaps students could prepare some of them at home and bring back to class to sample, if time is a factor in preparing them in class.

20. Create a pretend door for your students to stand behind. When they say a certain chant or saying like Hannah did, ("ready or not, here I come...") they could be transported to another location where they can pretend they live. This could be a great way to assimilate social studies topics.

WORD SEARCH - *The Devil's Arithmetic*

All the words in this list are associated with *The Devil's Arithmetic*. The words are placed backwards, forward, diagonally, up and down. The included words are listed below the word search.

```
B A B U S H K A S Q N B H L Q Y T T J C D W N G
S Z Y R C Y Y N H C S U D M V V A B V W X I E M
C B D T H D O L M S A R C X D C I R X M Q N W C
H A N N A H B L U E I N K A F I K O M A N E R N
N A G M N R E C E B N E O O U A Z N S U Y F O C
E X G J U E I A L N L D P P M L Y X L K L Y C Y
L F X G K S L T L O P I S R Y M D G M G G K H V
L F O C A N S I H T T Y N W O L A R E K I B E H
F S Y U H D L E J M H H I Q Z C Z N O J T Z L S
X B I B R 1 A Z L A E Y E T T D E V D N L C L N
S E D E R W 9 H Z M H T I S Z D B S K O S H E R
N X D X T F O 4 H I E E I C B C P K S L S O S V
N M I D G Q S L 2 D A N A C E A H Y B E H S H G
P G S H W C P M F D A X G S S C S A P R D E O L
T R H P A S S O V E R T A T T O O K K M E N R Z
H O L O C A U S T N O Q M R W E Z L E V F U N T
A U N T E V A P S T N R C F M O R K D T V T R D
```

1942	CHOSEN	KOSHER	TWO
AARON	CLOTHES BASKET	LUBLIN	VIOSK
AFIKOMAN	EASTER	MIDDEN	WINE
ARITHMETIC	ELIJAH	MUSSELMEN	WOLFE
AUNT EVA	FAYGE	NEW ROCHELLE	YARMULKES
BABUSHKA	FOUR	PASSOVER	YIDDISH
BLUE INK	GITL	PROCESSED	YITZCHAK
BREUR	HAGGADAH	SCHNELL	YOLEN
BRONX	HANNAH	SEDER	
BURNED	HEALTHY	SHMUEL	
CANOPY	HOLOCAUST	SHORN	
CAULDRONS	ICE COLD	SKY	
CHANUKAH	KOMMANDOS	TATTOO	

All the words in this list are associated with *The Devil's Arithmetic*. The words are placed backwards, forward, diagonally, up and down. The included words are listed below the word search.

```
B A B U S H K A S       B           Y               W N
S       C Y       H C   U         V A B           I E
C       H   O L M   A R C           I R           N W
H A N N A H B L U E I N K A F I K O M A N E R       O
N A   M N R E C E B   E O O U A   N S U             C
E   G   U E I A L N L D P P M L Y X     K L       G K H
L F   G K S L T L O   I   R Y M D G       G K     H E
L   O   A   S I H T T Y N   O   A R E       I     E
    Y U H D   E J M H H I       C   N O     T     L S
    I   R 1 A   L A E Y E T     E   D N L C   L
S E D E R W 9 H   M H T I S Z     S K O S H E R
    D       O 4   I E E I C B C   K S   S O S
    I       L 2 D A N A C E A H Y B E     S H
    S       F D A     S   C S A   R D E O
    H P A S S O V E R T A T T O O K K   E N R
H O L O C A U S T N O       W E   L E     U N
A U N T E V A       N         O R   D T     R
```

1942
AARON
AFIKOMAN
ARITHMETIC
AUNT EVA
BABUSHKA
BLUE INK
BREUR
BRONX
BURNED
CANOPY
CAULDRONS
CHANUKAH

CHOSEN
CLOTHES BASKET
EASTER
ELIJAH
FAYGE
FOUR
GITL
HAGGADAH
HANNAH
HEALTHY
HOLOCAUST
ICE COLD
KOMMANDOS

KOSHER
LUBLIN
MIDDEN
MUSSELMEN
NEW ROCHELLE
PASSOVER
PROCESSED
SCHNELL
SEDER
SHMUEL
SHORN
SKY
TATTOO

TWO
VIOSK
WINE
WOLFE
YARMULKES
YIDDISH
YITZCHAK
YOLEN

CROSSWORD - *The Devil's Arithmetic*

CROSSWORD CLUES - *Devil's Arithmetic*

ACROSS

1. Author

3. Carried Fayge to Lilith's Cave
6. Newcomers

7. Fayge's Polish village
9. Grandpa Will and Grandma Belle's residence
12. Hannah Stern's hometown; New____
14. Chaya's aunt
16. Annual Jewish feast

19. Butcher who escaped camp
22. Blue numbers burnt into flesh
24. Chaya's uncle who fails to escape the camp

25. Read by Aaron out of the Haggadah for the Seder; Four ____

28. Garbage pile where children hid
29. Done to Jews' hair
30. Used by a young Hannah to imitate her grandfather; blue ____
31. Temperature of showers
33. Made to work hard at the camp
35. Called Ron-ron by his big sister Hannah

36. To remember and tell so it won't happen again; bear ____

37. Where Aaron hid the afikoman; ____ basket
38. Those taken to the fire
39. Number of days spent in cattle cars

DOWN

1. Spoken & understood by Chaya Abramowicz
2. Chaya's home village before joining Gitl
3. Made Hannah's head hurt after she drank it
4. Chaya's friend Rivka; Aunt ____
5. Mass destruction of European Jews
8. Jews made to carry the corpses
10. Steal
11. Apartment door opened to welcome him
12. Removing Jews to the concentration camps
13. Gas ovens; Lilith's ____
15. Number of villagers to survive camp
17. Matzoh wrapped in blue cloth and hidden
18. Fayge's rabbi father; Reb ____
19. Little hats worn by men during ceremony
20. Time travels to Polish village in 1940s
21. Permitted according to Jewish law
23. Hitler's plan to rid Jews; ____ Solution
26. Sang around the smokestack
27. God's canopy
29. Yelled constantly to the Jews at camp
31. Fayge and Shmuel were married under one
32. Christian holiday celebrated by Rosemary
34. Nazi camp comandant

CROSSWORD ANSWER KEY - *The Devil's Arithmetic*

Grid answers:

YOLEN

WOLFE

ZUGANGI

VIOSK

BRONX

NEAL

ROCHELLE

GITL

PASSOVER

YITZCHAK

TATTOO

SHMUEL

QUESTIONS

MIDDEN

SHORN

INK

COLD

HEALTHY

AARON

WITNESS

CLOTHES

CHOSEN

FOUR

MATCHING QUIZ/WORKSHEET 1 - *The Devil's Arithmetic*

_____ 1. YOLEN   A. Made to work hard at the camp

_____ 2. CLOTHES BASKET   B. Newcomers

_____ 3. FAYGE   C. Sang around the smokestack

_____ 4. HOLOCAUST   D. Shmuel's fiance

_____ 5. PASSOVER   E. Those taken to the fire

_____ 6. CHOSEN   F. Number of days spent in the cattle cars

_____ 7. CAULDRONS   G. Author

_____ 8. CHANUKAH   H. One plus one; each day alive

_____ 9. AUNT EVA   I. Done to Jews' hair

_____ 10. SHORN   J. Garbage pile where children hid

_____ 11. MIDDEN   K. Fayge's rabbi father

_____ 12. NEW ROCHELLE   L. Huge soup kettles

_____ 13. FOUR   M. God's canopy

_____ 14. ZUGANGI   N. Chaya's friend Rivka

_____ 15. HEALTHY   O. Eight day Jewish festival held in December

_____ 16. SWALLOWS   P. Permitted according to Jewish law

_____ 17. REB BORUCH   Q. Annual Jewish feast

_____ 18. SKY   R. Hannah Stern's hometown

_____ 19. KOSHER   S. Mass destruction of European Jews

_____ 20. ARITHMETIC   T. Where Aaron hid the afikoman

KEY: MATCHING QUIZ/WORKSHEET 1 - *The Devil's Arithmetic*

G - 1. YOLEN   A. Made to work hard at the camp

T - 2. CLOTHES BASKET   B. Newcomers

D - 3. FAYGE   C. Sang around the smokestack

S - 4. HOLOCAUST   D. Shmuel's fiance

Q - 5. PASSOVER   E. Those taken to the fire

E - 6. CHOSEN   F. Number of days spent in the cattle cars

L - 7. CAULDRONS   G. Author

O - 8. CHANUKAH   H. One plus one; each day alive

N - 9. AUNT EVA   I. Done to Jews' hair

I - 10. SHORN   J. Garbage pile where children hid

J - 11. MIDDEN   K. Fayge's rabbi father

R - 12. NEW ROCHELLE   L. Huge soup kettles

F - 13. FOUR   M. God's canopy

B - 14. ZUGANGI   N. Chaya's friend Rivka

A - 15. HEALTHY   O. Eight day Jewish festival held in December

C - 16. SWALLOWS   P. Permitted according to Jewish law

K - 17. REB BORUCH   Q. Annual Jewish feast

M - 18. SKY   R. Hannah Stern's hometown

P - 19. KOSHER   S. Mass destruction of European Jews

H - 20. ARITHMETIC   T. Where Aaron hid the afikoman

MATCHING QUIZ/WORKSHEET 2 - *The Devil's Arithmetic*

____ 1. AFIKOMAN   A. God's canopy

____ 2. BRONX   B. Matzoh wrapped in blue cloth and hidden

____ 3. ELIJAH   C. Permitted according to Jewish law

____ 4. PASSOVER   D. Means order

____ 5. SEDER   E. Kommando Wolfe as a boy

____ 6. MUSSELMEN   F. Grandpa Will and Grandma Belle's residence

____ 7. GRANDPA WILL   G. Made to work hard at the camp

____ 8. KOSHER   H. Annual Jewish feast

____ 9. SCHNELL   I. Chaya's aunt

____ 10. SKY   J. Yelled constantly to the Jews at the camp

____ 11. GITL   K. Time travels to Polish village in 1940's

____ 12. FOUR   L. Chaya's friend Rivka

____ 13. AUNT EVA   M. Number of days spent in the cattle cars

____ 14. WOLFE   N. Showers

____ 15. EASTER   O. Christian holiday celebrated by Rosemary

____ 16. HANNAH   P. Apartment door opened to welcome him

____ 17. LILITH'S CAVE   Q. Carried Fayge to Lilith's Cave

____ 18. HEALTHY   R. Fayge's rabbi father

____ 19. REB BORUCH   S. Those who give up the fight

____ 20. ICE COLD   T. Gas ovens

KEY: MATCHING QUIZ/WORKSHEET 2 - *The Devil's Arithmetic*

B - 1. AFIKOMAN

F - 2. BRONX

P - 3. ELIJAH

H - 4. PASSOVER

D - 5. SEDER

S - 6. MUSSELMEN

E - 7. GRANDPA WILL

C - 8. KOSHER

J - 9. SCHNELL

A - 10. SKY

I - 11. GITL

M - 12. FOUR

L - 13. AUNT EVA

Q - 14. WOLFE

O - 15. EASTER

K - 16. HANNAH

T - 17. LILITH'S CAVE

G - 18. HEALTHY

R - 19. REB BORUCH

N - 20. ICE COLD

A. God's canopy

B. Matzoh wrapped in blue cloth and hidden

C. Permitted according to Jewish law

D. Means order

E. Kommando Wolfe as a boy

F. Grandpa Will and Grandma Belle's residence

G. Made to work hard at the camp

H. Annual Jewish feast

I. Chaya's aunt

J. Yelled constantly to the Jews at the camp

K. Time travels to Polish village in 1940's

L. Chaya's friend Rivka

M. Number of days spent in the cattle cars

N. Showers

O. Christian holiday celebrated by Rosemary

P. Apartment door opened to welcome him

Q. Carried Fayge to Lilith's Cave

R. Fayge's rabbi father

S. Those who give up the fight

T. Gas ovens

SCRAMBLED	WORD	CLUE
DIISHYD	YIDDISH	Spoken and understood by Chaya Abramowicz
AKDNOOMSM	KOMMANDOS	Jews made to carry the corpses
ETNLEEESTTMR	RESETTLEMENT	Removing Jews to the concentration camps
APSOESRV	PASSOVER	Annual Jewish feast
ETRSEA	EASTER	Christian holiday celebrated by Rosemary
AOTOTT	TATTOO	Blue numbers burnt into flesh
MYSEKUALR	YARMULKES	Little hats worn by men during ceremony
TULLIOOSINNAF	FINAL SOLUTION	Hitler's plan to rid Jews
ZKACHYTI	YITZCHAK	Butcher who escaped camp
HYEHLAT	HEALTHY	Made to work hard at the camp
KYS	SKY	God's canopy
NSTEUOSFRUIQO	FOUR QUESTIONS	Read by Aaron out of the Haggadah for the Seder
NHAANH	HANNAH	Time travels to Polish village in 1940's
KNCULCGI	CLUCKING	Warning sound to children to hide
EGFAY	FAYGE	Shmuel's fiance
APDWALLGRIN	GRANDPA WILL	Kommando Wolfe as a boy
UINBLL	LUBLIN	Chaya's home village before joining Gitl
RDESE	SEDER	Means order
KNHACAUH	CHANUKAH	Eight day Jewish festival held in December
SMSENULME	MUSSELMEN	Those who give up the fight
LIHAEJ	ELIJAH	Apartment door opened to welcome him
LASTVHILLE'IC	LILITH'S CAVE	Gas ovens
HBRCEORUB	REB BORUCH	Fayge's rabbi father
UNGIZAG	ZUGANGI	Newcomers
LAYTHEH	HEALTHY	Made to work hard at the camp
XNRBO	BRONX	Grandpa Will and Grandma Belle's residence
SDLCUNARO	CAULDRONS	Huge soup kettles
LTIG	GITL	Chaya's aunt
NPAYOC	CANOPY	Fayge and Shmuel were to be married under one

VOCABULARY RESOURCE MATERIALS

VOCABULARY WORD SEARCH - *The Devil's Arithmetic*

All the words in this list are associated with *The Devil's Arithmetic* with emphasis on the vocabulary words being studied in the unit. The words are placed backwards, forward, diagonally, up and down. The included words are listed below the word search.

```
M E S M E R I Z E D D R X N B M O R T I F I E D
S R C G R U E S O M E A N P I T T L C B E N P T
U A S L D W B C K X S J L G L S V Q E G R J R X
N U J X O P W Y A F E J Y I L G T D V X V G O Z
L C O Q X Y F J M J C O M P E N S A T I O N F F
E O S N Y Q I K A G R R E Z T N S D C W R D O S
A U T P D L T N L A A B L D J A A O E C M O U S
V S L O V E N S G U T T U R A L R T N C A P N S
E D I R U E H W A D E F S R V U U B E O R T D Y
N I N T L D H U M Y K P I S N M I C I D R E O W
E S G E N V O E M V R J V D I I O M I T G O E B
D T A N E M J U M A I I E Q Z N S M P D R K U D
L O R T R L E W R E N G V M P O G H I U Y A F S
W R I S A X M A Q X N I O E X U L R E N D R R C
F T S D B N H H G N N C Z R T S M P A D O E W Y
D E H B L B I T M E P Q E E B E D X P T Q U N T
P D K B E W W C H J R G D B D Z D D K F E M S T
```

ALIENATED
AMALGAM
ARBITRARY
BILLET
BURNISHED
CLOYING
COMPENSATION
DECREED
DEHUMANIZED
DESECRATE
DISTORTED

DOUR
ELUSIVE
EXODUS
FERVOR
GARISH
GAUDY
GRUESOME
GUTTURAL
IMPUDENT
INGRATE
IRONY

JOSTLING
LUCID
LUMINOUS
MEAGER
MESMERIZED
MORTIFIED
OMINOUS
PORTENTS
PROFOUND
RAUCOUS
RIVETED

SATANIC
SLOVENS
SONOROUS
STACCATO
UNLEAVENED
VEHEMENCE
VIGOR
VULNERABLE

KEY: VOCABULARY WORD SEARCH - *The Devil's Arithmetic*

All the words in this list are associated with *The Devil's Arithmetic* with emphasis on the vocabulary words being studied in the unit. The words are placed backwards, forward, diagonally, up and down. The included words are listed below the word search.

```
M E S M E R I Z E D D         B M O R T I F I E D
  R C G R U E S O M E A       I         E     P
U A   L               S   L   L S     E     R     R
N U J     O       A   E     I L   T       X V     O
L C O         Y     M   C O M P E N S A T I O N   F
E O S           I   A G R   E   T N S D C   R D O
A U T P D     N L A A B L     A A O E C     O U
V S L O V E N S G U T T U R A L R T N C     N S
E D I R U E H   A D E   S R   U U B E O R T D Y
N I N T L D H U M Y     I   N M I C I D R E O
E S G E N   O E M V R   V   I I O M I T   O E
D T A N E M   U M A I I E   N S M P D R   U D
  O R T R   E   R E N G V   O G H I U   A   S
  R I S A     A     N I O E U   R E N D   R
  T S   B N     G     C Z R T S   A D O E   Y
  E H   L   I     E     E E   E       T   U N
  D     E     C     R       D   D       E   S T
```

ALIENATED	DOUR	JOSTLING	SATANIC
AMALGAM	ELUSIVE	LUCID	SLOVENS
ARBITRARY	EXODUS	LUMINOUS	SONOROUS
BILLET	FERVOR	MEAGER	STACCATO
BURNISHED	GARISH	MESMERIZED	UNLEAVENED
CLOYING	GAUDY	MORTIFIED	VEHEMENCE
COMPENSATION	GRUESOME	OMINOUS	VIGOR
DECREED	GUTTURAL	PORTENTS	VULNERABLE
DEHUMANIZED	IMPUDENT	PROFOUND	
DESECRATE	INGRATE	RAUCOUS	
DISTORTED	IRONY	RIVETED	

VOCABULARY CROSSWORD - *The Devil's Arithmetic*

VOCABULARY CROSSWORD CLUES - *Devil's Arithmetic*

ACROSS

1. Deformed; twisted
5. bouncing; bumping
7. Threatening
9. Of Satan
11. Clear-headed
15. Departure; exit
16. Skimpy
18. Erratic; inconsistent
20. Contradiction
21. Energy
24. Heated emotion
27. Throaty; gravelly
31. Made without yeast
33. Heavy; penetrating
34. Hypnotized; captivated
35. Loud, abrupt sounds

DOWN

1. Ruin; violate
2. Sour; gloomy
3. Shyness
4. Benefits
6. Cocky; arrogant
8. Unclean; untidy
10. Furnace used for cremation
12. Satisfying
13. Ordered
14. Humiliated
17. Reduction
19. Position
22. Loud; piercing
23. Distanced
25. Passion; intensity
26. Showy
27. Horrible
28. Attention drawn to
29. Shocked
30. Deep; full sounding
32. Puzzling; slippery

```
D I S T O R T E D   T   C         J O S T L I N G
E           O M I N O U S           M
S A T A N I C   U   M   M   L U C I D   M P
E       R   R   I   P   O   L   E X O D U S
C   M E A G E R     D   E   V   O   C   R D       C
R       M     I     N   E   Y   R   T   E       O
A R B I T R A R Y   T   S   N   I   E   I       M
T   I     T     Y   A   S   N   E   F   T       P
E   L   I R O N Y       T       G   D   I       R
    L     R       V I G O R   A   F E R V O R
    E     I   G   O     A   L   D   E       E
G U T T E R A L   A   N   U   I       H     S
R       I     U A   S   C   E       E       S
U N L E A V E N E D   P R O F O U N D     M   I
E   L   I     Y P R   N   U   A     E     O
S   U   T       A   O   S   T     N     N
O   S   E       L   R     E     C
M   I   D       L   O     D     E
E   V           E   U
    M E S M E R I Z E D   S T A C C A T O
```

_____ 1. DESECRATE   A. Ruin; violate

_____ 2. TIMIDITY   B. Loud; piercing

_____ 3. DISCERNIBLE   C. Ungrateful person

_____ 4. VULNERABLE   D. Reduction

_____ 5. GARISH   E. Unable to solve

_____ 6. ALIENATED   F. Unable to distinguish

_____ 7. EXODUS   G. Made without yeast

_____ 8. UNLEAVENED   H. Departure; exit

_____ 9. DISSIPATING   I. Puzzling; slippery

_____ 10. COMPRESSION   J. Defenseless; exposed

_____ 11. RAUCOUS   K. Shyness

_____ 12. DOUR   L. Recognizable

_____ 13. COMPENSATION   M. One image on top of another

_____ 14. INGRATE   N. Tasteless; gaudy

_____ 15. OMINOUS   O. Benefits

_____ 16. UNDECIPHERABLE   P. Sour; gloomy

_____ 17. UNDISTINGUISHABLE   Q. Disappearing

_____ 18. INDELIBLE   R. Distances

_____ 19. ELUSIVE   S. Threatening

_____ 20. SUPERIMPOSED   T. Permanent; unforgetting

KEY: VOCABULARY WORKSHEET 1 - *The Devil's Arithmetic*

A - 1. DESECRATE

K - 2. TIMIDITY

L - 3. DISCERNIBLE

J - 4. VULNERABLE

N - 5. GARISH

R - 6. ALIENATED

H - 7. EXODUS

G - 8. UNLEAVENED

Q - 9. DISSIPATING

D - 10. COMPRESSION

B - 11. RAUCOUS

P - 12. DOUR

O - 13. COMPENSATION

C - 14. INGRATE

S - 15. OMINOUS

E - 16. UNDECIPHERABLE

F - 17. UNDISTINGUISHABLE

T - 18. INDELIBLE

I - 19. ELUSIVE

M - 20. SUPERIMPOSED

A. Ruin; violate

B. Loud; piercing

C. Ungrateful person

D. Reduction

E. Unable to solve

F. Unable to distinguish

G. Made without yeast

H. Departure; exit

I. Puzzling; slippery

J. Defenseless; exposed

K. Shyness

L. Recognizable

M. One image on top of another

N. Tasteless; gaudy

O. Benefits

P. Sour; gloomy

Q. Disappearing

R. Distances

S. Threatening

T. Permanent; unforgetting

_____ 1. CONSPIRATORIAL

_____ 2. DISTORTED

_____ 3. COMPENSATION

_____ 4. PERVASIVE

_____ 5. DEHUMANIZED

_____ 6. COMPRESSION

_____ 7. PORTENTS

_____ 8. BURNISHED

_____ 9. MORTIFIED

_____ 10. ALIENATED

_____ 11. COMPANIONABLE

_____ 12. CREMATORIA

_____ 13. GUTTURAL

_____ 14. INDELIBLE

_____ 15. LUMINOUS

_____ 16. MEAGER

_____ 17. ROUTINIZATION

_____ 18. AMALGAM

_____ 19. RAUCOUS

_____ 20. ELUSIVE

A. Deformed; twisted

B. Throaty; gravelly

C. Puzzling; slippery

D. Polished; waxed

E. Humiliated

F. Friendly; agreeable

G. Benefits

H. Bright; shining

I. Deprived of human dignity

J. Skimpy

K. Secretly plotting

L. Loud; piercing

M. Permanent; unforgetting

N. Indications; omens

O. Furnace used for cremation

P. Widespread

Q. Distances

R. Put into a system

S. Reduction

T. Mixture

KEY: VOCABULARY WORKSHEET 2 - *The Devil's Arithmetic*

K - 1. CONSPIRATORIAL

A - 2. DISTORTED

G - 3. COMPENSATION

P - 4. PERVASIVE

I - 5. DEHUMANIZED

S - 6. COMPRESSION

N - 7. PORTENTS

D - 8. BURNISHED

E - 9. MORTIFIED

Q - 10. ALIENATED

F - 11. COMPANIONABLE

O - 12. CREMATORIA

B - 13. GUTTURAL

M - 14. INDELIBLE

H - 15. LUMINOUS

J - 16. MEAGER

R - 17. ROUTINIZATION

T - 18. AMALGAM

L - 19. RAUCOUS

C - 20. ELUSIVE

A. Deformed; twisted

B. Throaty; gravelly

C. Puzzling; slippery

D. Polished; waxed

E. Humiliated

F. Friendly; agreeable

G. Benefits

H. Bright; shining

I. Deprived of human dignity

J. Skimpy

K. Secretly plotting

L. Loud; piercing

M. Permanent; unforgetting

N. Indications; omens

O. Furnace used for cremation

P. Widespread

Q. Distances

R. Put into a system

S. Reduction

T. Mixture

SCRAMBLED	WORD	CLUE
RHYREEIPP	PERIPHERY	Edge; fringe
EOLAPCNBIONMA	COMPANIONABLE	Friendly; agreeable
CDLEIHBNEERPUA	UNDECIPHERABLE	Unable to solve
RSIONAATOLPIRC	CONSPIRATORIAL	Secretly plotting
TNPDAIGISSI	DISSIPATING	Disappearing
RFMDETIOI	MORTIFIED	Humiliated
OIGLYCN	CLOYING	Satisfying
NCNOIRNTAIEI	INCINERATION	Burning
AEREMG	MEAGER	Skimpy
DUYGA	GAUDY	Showy
VOEFRR	FERVOR	Heated emotion
ISEUVEL	ELUSIVE	Puzzling; slippery
UMEORSEG	GRUESOME	Horrible
SUOONIM	OMINOUS	Threatening
YITIIMTD	TIMIDITY	Shyness
BLNSIDCEREI	DISCERNIBLE	Recognizable
OASTATCC	STACCATO	Loud, abrupt sounds
OESNSVL	SLOVENS	Unclean; untidy
TAIAFRIMONF	AFFIRMATION	Approval
ACNONSTOMEPI	COMPENSATION	Benefits
IUISISGDLAENUBTNH	UNDISTINGUISHABLE	Unable to distinguish
TENIPUDM	IMPUDENT	Cocky; arrogant
OURD	DOUR	Sour; gloomy
ZMEEIMSEDR	MESMERIZED	Hypnotized; captivated
LAMAMAG	AMALGAM	Mixture
ARGSHI	GARISH	Tasteless; gaudy
BRRYATIRA	ARBITRARY	Erratic; inconsistent
HZMEDDEANIU	DEHUMANIZED	Deprived of human dignity
NEATGIR	INGRATE	Ungrateful person
OTREIRMACA	CREMATORIA	Furnace used for cremation
ASATCNI	SATANIC	Of Satan
CDEARESET	DESECRATE	Ruin; violate
YNIOR	IRONY	Contradiction